How to Become a
Successful Commercial Model

How to Become a Successful Commercial

Model

Table Of Contents

■   ■   ■   ■   ■

Read This Before Beginning The Book

I would like to thank and congratulate you for purchasing this book. You have now taken the most important step in getting the needed information to become a successful commercial model.

This took me four years to complete. I have condensed more than a decade's worth of my experience as a working professional actor and commercial model into a practical, informative, fun and valuable book that will greatly benefit you whether you are pursuing commercial modeling as a hobby or as a full-time occupation.

While reading the book, please think of questions that you would like to have answered. They can be general questions about the industry or specific ones that pertain to improving your career. I will try to personally answer as many questions as possible.

You and I will greatly benefit from this individualized service. I am offering you a free, honest and straightforward response to your questions. In return, your questions will teach me what additional information is desired. This allows me to keep my seminar and *How to Become a Successful Commercial Model Newsletter* up-to-date and informative. As a token of my appreciation, I will give a free copy of the newsletter to those whose questions are used in the newsletter. Upon request, names will be withheld.

Mail your questions or comments to:
The Marcus Institute of Commercial Modeling, Aaron Marcus, Director
P.O. Box 32564 Baltimore, MD 21282-2564 or e-mail bk@howtomodel.com
web site: http://www.how to model.com

If you would like more information about my seminar or newsletter, please write to me at the above address.

Thanks again for your purchase and I hope you enjoy this book.

Sincerely,

Aaron Marcus

■　■　■　■　■

For Nancy

Acknowledgments

Editors: Mark Littmann
          Laurie Mazur

Typesetting: Brushwood Graphics, Inc.

Cover Design: Phylis Randal—The Image Factory

A special thank you to Mark, Laurie, Jeff Goldman, and Pam. Without your kindness, wisdom, and encouragement, this project would not have happened.

Cover Photo: Bill Simone—Simone Associates, Inc. (717) 274-3621

Model: Laurie Martin

Makeup: Jean D'Orazio

Eileen Needham & Arthur Bronfin (McDonald/Richards Model Management) I can't thank you enough for giving me a chance.

Jeremy & Jennifer: For being the most wonderful children any dad could ask for.

■ ■ ■ ■ ■

Introduction

When most people think of modeling, they only think of **fashion** models—those tall, thin, glamorous men and women who appear in ads for designer clothes. But you don't need to look like Kate Moss, Cindy Crawford, or Joel West to succeed as a model.

Commercial models, who appear in ads for everything from toothpaste to insurance, come in all shapes, sizes and ages. Some are gorgeous and handsome, however, many successful commercial models look just like everyday people. The individual who has the greatest chance of being chosen to appear in an ad is the one who can believably look like a mom, doctor, business person, plumber, student, grandparent, teacher, dad, etc. Although there are many beautiful and handsome commercial models, it is not necessary to have that "perfect" look in order to be successful.

This book will explain the best ways to:

- Get started—by teaching you specific techniques to help you practice looking comfortable and believable in front of a still camera.
- Make contacts—by learning how to find literally thousands of agents, photographers, and art directors.
- Grab the attention of agents—by discovering what they want to see in head shots and composite sheets.
- Learn techniques—to help you get cast at go-sees.
- Find work on your own.
- Accurately manage and understand the business side of commercial modeling.

As in any business, there are no guarantees in commercial modeling. However, being prepared and extremely knowledgeable gives you the greatest chance for success.

■ ■ ■ ■ ■

What Is Commercial Modeling?

What are commercial models used for?

Every day you see commercial models in many different types of ads. They appear in newspapers, catalogs, magazines, editorials, (photos shown in conjunction with an article in a magazine), brochures, on posters, billboards, sides of buses, packages of food items, household products, games, etc.

The commercial model is the silent salesperson promoting a product or company. He or she has to act without words.

To even be considered as a *fashion* model you must have very specific physical requirements. Normally female fashion models are between 5'10" and 6' tall and must wear a size six to eight. Male fashion models are normally 6' to 6'2" tall and wear a size 40 regular jacket.

Commercial models, on the other hand, need only to have the ability to look like a real person. In commercial modeling people of all heights, weights, sizes, ages, and races are hired. Fashion models normally promote high-end designer clothes; commercial models advertise everything else.

The commercial model connects the client, product and the consumer. A client is the person whose product needs to be advertised. Usually, the client hires an ad agency to produce an ad, the ad agency hires the photographer, and either the art director from the ad agency or photographer hires the commercial model through the model's agent.

How much do commercial models earn?

The fees are different from city to city and job to job. Adult commercial models can expect to make anywhere from $50 to $250 an hour depending on the market. Children are paid less than adults, but can earn up to $75 an hour. There is no way of knowing how much one can earn. I know a commercial model who earned $50,000 from one job, and I know people who have made $2,000 for an entire year.

■   ■   ■   ■   ■

Most people do not realize that commercial modeling is like any other kind of business. Before entering this or any industry, you must do your homework. You must learn about the types of photos that will get you the most work. You must understand what agents do, and know how to make sure you are working with a reputable and honest agent. You must know what is expected of you as a professional model, and learn how to practice before entering the business. Certainly, the people who have done their research and have gotten the needed information will have the greatest chance for success.

What does it take to make it as a commercial model?

The best way to get work as a commercial model is to learn some acting skills, be self-motivated, and have the time to accept work.

How do models get work?

This process is explained in great detail in the book. The short answer is that agents send models' composite sheets (a collection of photos) to a photographer or art director, and he or she decides which model to hire for the job. Sometimes models audition for the job by attending a *go-see*: models go to a photographer's studio or casting office and they are seen.

What are the advantages to working as a commercial model?

As I mentioned earlier there are no physical limitations to being a commercial model. Most people do commercial modeling to supplement their income on a part-time basis. The hours are extremely flexible, and the hourly fees paid to commercial models are wonderful. And, of course, it is a thrill to see yourself or your child in a magazine, newspaper, brochure, or on a poster or billboard.

What are the disadvantages?

There is no guarantee that there will be steady work. That is why most people work part-time. There are no health benefits, and no money is withheld from your checks for tax purposes. You are responsible for paying taxes on all income.

What does it take to get started?

A person can get started by simply having a head shot taken. In the book I explain how to get photos taken free as well as how to find professional photographers to shoot your head shots. Depending on the area, one can have a head shot taken and begin trying to get work for about $350. Finding agents to submit your head shot for jobs would be the next best step. It is important to get experience working in front of a camera before trying to work in a major market.

2

Preparation For Commercial Modeling

Acting Lessons

A commercial model must be able to act without words. Acting lessons can give you the tools.

Acting lessons can teach you how to re-experience emotions, to recreate events and situations from your past, and to have the skill to bring them to the present. You must be able to feel emotions in front of a camera and quickly switch them.

I am not going to discuss acting methods, but I would like to share one technique that helps me get into character while working in front of a camera. The technique involves talking to the camera or the other model while shooting.

Talk about the product. Bring the words and message of the ad alive with your actions. For example: you are doing an ad for insulation. The ad is trying to convey that when you use insulation in your home you feel warmer in the winter, cooler in the summer and your utility bills will be lower. You are holding a package of insulation in your hands, and you might say one of these short sentences. "This stuff is great. My house stays so warm in the winter. I'm saving money on my heating bill. It's incredible." The way to make yourself believe what you are saying, which will make everyone looking at the ad believe you, is to connect the words with something real in your life. Even if insulation does not matter to you, there is something that you own or would like to own that will make you more comfortable. Think of that object during the shoot.

If talking is not appropriate, then think the words to yourself. Imagine you are working on an ad where a bank wants to show how pleasant, friendly, and helpful its employees are. Your character is the customer at the other bank in town. You can't get your questions answered. It takes a long time before someone even tries to help you. Try to remember a real experience where you were not treated well. If you are asked to recreate emotions that you have never experienced, then you should make up different scenarios in order to believably feel and portray them.

■ ■ ■ ■ ■

One of the exciting things about commercial modeling is being able to play different characters. One day you can be a nerd, the next day, the president of a corporation.

Commercial models must be able to understand the concept of an ad, take direction from an art director or photographer and produce the look on the spot. The next two pages show examples from real shoots where I had to feel different emotions and display them convincingly.

A nationally known science museum was promoting a film called Antarctica. In the ad you see a man (me) dressed for summer. I am wearing a Hawaiian shirt and watching the Antarctica film. The film is so realistic that you feel like you are there.

Because it is so cold in Antarctica, I have a windburned face, ice forming on my chin, snow on my feet, and penguins standing next to me.

Here is the tricky part. If I look like I am freezing, the shot doesn't work. The museum doesn't want people to think that they will feel uncomfortable if they attend the film. The photographer wanted me to look cold, but in a pleasant way.

How did I do that? I brought back memories of wonderful times I had in very cold environments: skiing, sledding, playing with my family in the snow. The next page shows the final ad.

Photo by Steve Pollock—Franklin Institute

Here's another example of the need to show different emotions. Imagine a business person sitting at a desk. The computer is slow; papers pile up. The project must be completed by the next day. Now your phone isn't working. The model must show frustration, anger, exhaustion, etc. In these situations I would tap into events from my past where I felt those emotions. The next two pages show some samples from different jobs where those types of emotions were needed.

Save Something A Lot More Valuable.

Photo by Bob Jones—Crestar Bank

If you are ever working with an animal always ask if it is a professionally trained animal. If it is not, you run a much higher risk of an accident taking place on the set. The monkey in this photo bit the assistant photographer. As it turned out, the monkey was just a pet and not properly trained.

Photo by Tony Sylvestro

This a very "glamorous" editorial shot for an article about hemorrhoids. As you can see, if I did not look like I was really uncomfortable the shot wouldn't work.

Photo by Mahomad Samia

Sometimes models are asked to show a caricature or highly exaggerated look instead of a real expression. That means making the character look almost cartoonish. Emotions must be blown up to such a level that the anger, frustration or happiness looks humorous or silly.

Here is a photo for an ad using a caricature format.

Photo by Bill Simone

To do a caricature you must be able to reproduce the basic feeling, then completely let go and make the shot look cartoonish. The photographer or art director will let you know if you are heading in the right direction.

The following two pages show examples of different types of emotions used for jobs.

Different types of emotions shown in ads

Photo by Herb Cosby

Photo by Paul Fetters Photography

Photo by Richard Ustinich

Photo by Stuart Zolotorow—Nancy Klein

Photo by Tony Sylvestro

Photo by Steve Biver

Photo by Len Rizzi

Photo by Joe Toto

In case you are wondering, I was not in a can for this ad on the right. The can was shot separately. Along with the print ad, I was also cast for the national TV commercial where an actual can was built for me to stand in.

Looking Comfortable in Front of a Still Camera

To help you practice looking comfortable and believable in front of the camera, make a list of different expressions and emotions. The most commonly used expressions in advertising are happiness, anger, frustration, love, feeling sick, confusion, and caring. Then, think of situations that will help you feel them. For example, if I wanted to practice looking happy, I would need to ask myself what kind of happiness I am feeling. Am I happy because I won the $20 million lottery, or because I got an A on my exam, or because I just got engaged? Next, I would think of an experience from my past that would allow me to feel the emotion needed for the proper look. If I needed to feel the excitement of winning a race, I could think about the time I hit a grand slam in a Little League all-star game. If you do not have any appropriate experiences, use your imagination.

Now you have a list of emotions and you have figured out ways of retrieving them. The next step is to have a friend or relative take pictures of you. You can use any kind of camera; even the cheapest Instamatic will do for this exercise. Just make sure that the photos are clear and your body and face can be easily seen. Have the list of emotions nearby, and work on one at a time. Try to remember the situation that will put you in touch with that feeling. A video camera can also be used. Study the photos or tape, and see where you were successful and where more work is needed.

Here are some other helpful techniques to use while practicing. It is best to look away from the camera while you are preparing yourself. That way there is less chance of the photographer accidentally taking your photo before you are ready, and it is easier to concentrate. Look at the ground or at a wall away from the camera. When you are ready, look straight into the lens of the camera. When on a professional modeling job, there are times when the photographer will ask you not to look directly into the lens, but most of the time models are asked to look straight into the camera. If you are planning to look away from the camera, make sure you find a spot to use as a landmark, so you can get your head in precisely the same position after each photo is taken. If you want to look just to the left of the camera, then find a place on the wall, or the edge of the camera to use as your mark. Whenever you look away from the lens, it is very difficult to consistently place your head in the same spot without a focus point.

Take acting classes and learn techniques that allow you to grab hold of different feelings. Mastering these skills will give you many different looks. Having access to a wide variety of expressions will make work enjoyable and challenging. Being able to take direction and translate thoughts and feelings into facial and body expressions will make you a more versatile and marketable model.

3

Head Shots

The next step in becoming a commercial model is to have a head shot taken. Head shots are generally a close-up photo of your face from your shoulders to the top of your head. Some people get commercial modeling jobs with only a head shot. In fact, that is how I got started.

Composite sheets, the model's business card, which are discussed later, will generally have one head shot photo. Also, many commercial models work as actors, and head shots are an essential tool of their trade.

It is important to understand what is needed to produce a great head shot. People want to see warm, inviting and interesting looks. It should capture your personality or the personality you want to project. A head shot should not be too dramatic. Avoid jewelry and clothes that are distracting. You want people to focus on your face.

Photo by Arthur Cohen Photography—
Jean Arbeiter
East Coast Style

Photo by Michael Papo Photography—
Jeff Chapman
West Coast Style

■   ■   ■   ■   ■

Have the photo taken by a photographer who understands the look you are trying to achieve. A more relaxed, natural setting, casual, West Coast look might not
be right for the more conservative East Coast. Make sure your photographer understands what look is desired for your area. In the next chapter I discuss how to find a
photographer for your head shot.

Styles change, but today most people choose matte finish prints (non-shiny) as
opposed to a glossy finish (shiny). 8 x 10 is the standard size for a head shot.

One last comment about head shots. Some people are moving away from the
traditional head shot, which is a close up shot from the shoulder to the top of the
head. Instead, many people are having a half or three-quarter body shot taken. This
shows much more of the person than a tight shot of the face.

Photo by Mary Ann Halpin (Halpin-Croyle Photography)—
Constance Zimmer

Photo by Mary Ann Halpin (Halpin-Croyle Photography)—
Steve Hughes

Resumes

If you are interested in acting as well as commercial modeling, you will need a one page resume stapled to the back of your 8 x 10 head shot. The resume gives specific information about you that is needed when auditioning for an acting job.

Here is an example of what a resume should look like.

YOUR NAME

Union Affiliation (for example: AFTRA/SAG)

Phone number (or agents)   Work number (optional) 555-1234   Pager number

Height: 5'7"
Weight: 143 lbs.
Age Range: (optional) 20–26
Eyes: Blue
Hair: Blonde

THEATER:

Name of Play	Character	Company
Hamlet	Hamlet	Arena Stage

FILM/TELEVISION:

Name of Film	Character	Studio
Gone With the Mind	Teacher	M.G.M.

COMMERCIALS—RADIO/TELEVISION:

Credits Available Upon Request

SPECIAL SKILLS:

Examples:

Dialects	Athlete (list sports)	Comedian
Musician (list instruments)	Dancer (list styles)	Motorcycle

TRAINING AND EDUCATION:

Examples:

B.S. (Theater) University of Such and Such	Stanislavski Techniques: Harry Stanis
Comedy: John Smith	Voice: Jane Song

■ ■ ■ ■ ■

The resume should include your:

- Name (and possibly your agent's name)
- Union affiliation—There are three unions affiliated with acting in the United States.

Depending on the type of work you do, you could belong to one or all three unions.

AFTRA   American Federation of Television and Radio Artists (radio commercials, soap operas, disk jockeys, news people)

SAG   Screen Actors Guild (movies, TV commercials, some TV shows—if shot on film)

AEA   Actors Equity Association (theater)

ACTRA   Association of Canadian Television and Radio Artists (the Canadian union)

There is a new union for models called The Models Guild. It should not be listed on an acting resume. For more information about unions, see Chapter 12: "Resources."

- Height
- Weight
- Age range (range of ages you can portray)
- Hair color
- Eye color
- Experience:
  - Plays you have been in
  - Industrial, feature or independent films
  - Training (where you have studied)
  - Special skills (dialects, karate, juggling, musical instruments, etc.)

When you are listing your experiences you should include things other than acting experience. If you are a teacher, lawyer, veteran, doctor, police officer, mechanic, etc., make sure you put this information on your resume. If a film is being cast and police officers are needed, and your resume shows that you are a police officer, you may have a greater chance of being cast for the part. When you are first beginning, you might not have much information to put on your resume. List anything: high school plays, community or college theater, or any relevant acting experience.

List all of your training. Showing your training credits (classes or seminars) can greatly help your chances of getting a part even with little acting experience.

The only guideline is that you must be honest. Do not lie on your resume. A casting director once told me about an actor who came in to read for a part. She looked at his resume and noticed he had a certain play listed on his resume. It just so happened the casting director's husband had directed that play. She knew everyone in the cast, and knew that he was not in the play. She told him to leave her office and that he was never allowed to audition for anything she is casting. So, don't fib about your experiences.

Similarly, only list special skills that you are extremely proficient in. An agent once told me about a person who was cast for a job partly because she listed riding horses as a special skill.

While shooting the commercial the director learned that the model not only could not ride horses, but was scared to death of them. She was fired on the spot and immediately replaced.

Do not list the TV commercials you have appeared in. Instead, write "TV commercial list available upon request." This is to avoid the appearance of "product conflicts"—where a person appears in ads for competing products. If you were in a commercial for Nike 10 years ago, but had it listed on your resume, you might not be considered for a Reebok commercial because of a perceived conflict. The casting agent might think the spot is still airing. However, if nothing is listed, and you are asked if you have any TV commercials currently running that would be considered competition to Nike, you can honestly say no. Although there can be conflicts for print ads, it is not as strict as TV. It is not unusual for a commercial model to appear in a number of ads for competing products. Print ads should not be listed on your acting resume.

Your resume is a continuous work in progress. As you get more impressive jobs, or perhaps study with some well known teachers, you will want to replace the old listings with the updated information.

Print your resume on a piece of paper, not directly on the back of the head shot. This makes your resume more economical and easier to update. Staple all four corners of the resume to the back of your head shot. Most head shots are placed in a drawer or file cabinet, crammed in with hundreds of others. Unless the resume is carefully fastened, it could easily be torn off.

Remember, resumes are used exclusively by actors trying to get acting jobs. There are some exceptions in a few specific markets, but generally models do not use resumes.

The head shot and resume are your most basic work tools. Next you will need a composite sheet.

5

Composite Sheets

A composite sheet is a collection of photographs that shows the variety of ways you can look. The composite sheet, or "comp," is the key that unlocks the door to getting work. The primary way to get cast for a job is for an agent to submit your comp to a photographer or an art director. Comps are also used at go-sees.

The most basic composite sheet will have a head shot on one side and two different types of photos on the back. The most common size is 5 x 7. (see next page)

■ ■ ■ ■ ■

Front of 5 x 7 composite sheet

Back of 5 x 7 composite sheet

Joseph McLaughlin
212/465-2574

Photo by Arthur Cohen—Joseph McLaughlin

YOUR EYES WILL NOT BELIEVE THE RANGE OF AARON MARCUS!

There is no set rule on how a comp must look. The size, shape, and appearance of a card is limited only by the model's imagination.

HEIGHT: 6' 0"   HAIR: LT. BROWN
SUIT: 39L   EYES: BLUE
NECK/SLEEVE: 15 34/35 SAG/AFTRA
WAIST: 33   GOOD HANDS
INSEAM: 32   PROFESSIONAL GUITARIST
SHOE: 10   ALL SPORTS

AARON MARCUS

Expressions

MODELING & TALENT AGENCY, INC.
104 Church Street, Philadelphia, PA 19106
Phone: (215) 923-4420 • Fax: (215) 440-7179

Putting Together Your Composite Sheet

If you are just beginning in commercial modeling and do not have any photos for a composite sheet, or you have done some ads but aren't crazy about the photos, or you like the photos you have done but feel they are not selling you well, then you can create your own "ad" photos. Here's how.

Studying Successful Models' Composite Sheets

Ask agents, photographers, or art directors if they have any composite sheets in their files that they consider special.

Ask to see comps of successful models. Get input from everyone, but remember: you are the one who should make the final decision. If you desire a more distinctive look for the design of your composite sheet, find a graphic artist to help you.

A graphic artist might place some photos in unusual ways on the page, or use lines to make a border around the photos, or use a special typeface to give the comp an interesting look. Creating the design of the comp before your session will help the photographer determine the cropping or shape of the shots.

Finding the Right Look for You

Deciding on the image or images that fit you best might be the hardest part of the whole process of putting together a composite sheet. Ask agents, casting agents, photographers, art directors and friends how they see you being cast. Consider their input, but you need to make the final decision. You must figure out how you want to present yourself to the world. Are you a grandparent type? An athlete? Do you look right drinking beer around a campfire, or sitting behind an office desk—or both?

All comps should have at least a few of the following "looks":

- Sports activity
- Exercise
- Student or teacher
- Dad, mom, grandparent
- Business (non executive–manager type)
- Relationship (husband-wife, boyfriend-girlfriend, etc.)
- Body shots—if appropriate show hands, feet, legs, etc.
  (Some ads only show parts of the model's body.)

- Blue collar
- Executive
- Housewife
- Customer
- Outdoors
- Nurse or doctor
- Family

Think about the types of photos that would best display those images. To help with ideas, look through:

- Magazines
- Agents' talent books (these publications show photos of the models they work with)

■ Newspaper ads
■ Junk mail
■ Photographers' showcase books (photographers pay to have their work shown in the books to generate business for themselves) One directory is called the American Photographer Showcase. Another is called The Creative Black Book. The Workbook is also a wonderful publication. These books can be found in camera stores, art schools, some public libraries, and at advertising agencies.

Never use a logo or a brand name for example, (IBM or McDonald's) in your shot. It could prevent you from getting other jobs with a competitor.

Planning Your Shot

Since the shots for your composite sheet don't have words, make sure each photograph itself tells the story. Even better, create a photo that shows more than one story. If you want to present yourself as a mom and a businesswoman, the photo might show you walking up the steps to your house wearing a business suit, carrying a briefcase, while your child runs to meet you. Take your time and be creative in thinking of different scenarios for your shots.

Magazines are a great source of ideas. Find the magazine that will feature the look you want. For example: *Parents Magazine* is great for shots of parents and kids. For business images, look through investment magazines.

The ads can give you information on how to style the shot and what props are needed. Props are items placed on the set to make the ad look real. For example, if the ad is supposed to take place in an auto garage, tools, oil cans, towels, grease guns, and auto parts would be appropriate props.

After selecting the types of shots you want, show the samples to anyone connected to the modeling or advertising industry for feedback. If you have not contacted an agent, show your ideas to art directors at advertising agencies, or photographers. If you are trying to copy an existing ad, do not expect to be able to make an exact duplicate. You probably will not have the money or experience. Do the best you can at making the shot look like a **real ad.**

Hiring a Photographer

Get the names of photographers working in your area. Ask agents, art directors or other models for the names of their favorite photographers. If you do not have any contacts, call the American Society of Media Photographers (ASMP). Some ASMP members only photograph landscapes, wildlife, or portraits, but many shoot ads with models. There are 36 ASMP chapters throughout the United States. Call the national office in Princeton Junction, New Jersey, at (609) 799-8300, (www.asmp.org) and ask for the phone number of the chapter in your area.

Composite Sheets

Or, for around $18, you can purchase a membership directory from the national office that will give you the names, addresses, and phone numbers of all 5,000 photographers who are members of ASMP. The directory will have codes describing what type of photography each photographer shoots. A mailing list on labels can be purchased, but if you are just getting started I would not recommend making the investment. If you ever decide to try to work outside of the United States you can also get the names of members living abroad.

You might be able to get your photos free or at reduced cost if the photographer is willing to do the shoot as a test. Test shots are not ads. They are used for the photographer's and model's portfolios.

Here is an example of a test shot. Although this photo was shot as a test shot, an art director saw it on my composite sheet, bought it, and used it as an ad. Whether you hire a photographer for a photo session or do test shots, try to make the final product look like an ad.

Photo by Bill Schilling—Jeremy Marcus

Another way to get photos for your comp (and actually get paid) is to find a photographer who does stock photography. These are generic photographs that can be used for many purposes. Typical stock photos include images of a happy husband and wife looking at their newborn baby, or of a business person sitting at a desk. Companies use stock photography because it is less expensive to purchase (actually rent) a ready-made stock photo than to produce an original photograph.

You can find stock photography companies by consulting the Stock Photo Desk Book. This reference book, which can be found in most libraries, lists stock photography companies by state. You may then call these companies and ask for the names of photographers in your area who shoot stock photos.

WARNING! There are however, a few things to keep in mind before appearing in a stock shot. When a model is hired for a regular ad there are specific agreements on the amount of time the ad can run and where it will be used. The model is paid a specific amount of money based on that information. When a model is hired for a stock shot, he or she must sign a document allowing the photographer or stock company to run the photo anywhere and forever without the model receiving any additional fees. Your image could be used on billboards, posters, or on products. If you become closely identified with a certain product because of the ad in which a stock photo appears, you could lose out on other jobs for competing products. You can make money and get great tear sheets when doing stock shots, but you are taking the risk of possibly losing money in the future.

Another thing to consider before doing a stock shot is that you never know what type of ad your image may appear in. You could be portrayed as a drug addict, alcoholic, pregnant teenager, child abuser, or some other character you might not want to be associated with. I was told about a model whose stock photo was used in a newspaper ad that showed her as one of the employees for a phone sex 900 number.

Many agents discourage models from doing stock photography. Some stock companies will hire models directly, so the agents lose out on their commissions. If the model becomes associated with a certain product, the agent could lose commissions on future bookings. If the model becomes closely associated with a sleazy or controversial ad, it might be very difficult for the agent to find photographers or art directors interested in hiring the model for future jobs. That will also mean less income for the agent.

I decided to do these stock shots (shown on the next page) because I knew that the photos would be so memorable that I would actually get more work from them.

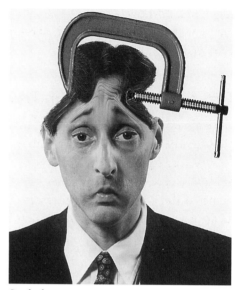

Stock photo by Barry Blackman, N.Y., N.Y.   *Stock photo* by Barry Blackman, N.Y., N.Y.

If hiring a professional photographer is not in your budget at this time, use your creativity. I have known models who found high school and college students taking photography classes to shoot the photos for their comps. The students loved having access to models to work with, and the models got very nice photos at little or no cost. One student actually used the photos for a class project. There are no guarantees that the photos will be usable for your comp. However, you could spend $500 at a professional photo session and still not get exactly what you need. Even if the photos don't work, the session will build your experience. Another advantage of going this route is that you never know where the photographer might end up in the industry. The photographer might become very successful and want to hire you again. Another inexpensive way of getting shots taken is by calling a number of local photographers and asking if they can recommend any assistant photographers. Assistant photographers are people who work as apprentices to more established photographers. They help the photographer adjust lights, build sets and load film into the camera. Many are trying to build their portfolios in order to get their own bookings. They may be in great need of models to work with. Once again, not only might you get some wonderful photos, but you may also make contact with an up-and-coming photographer who might remember you when he or she is casting for his or her next job.

Set up appointments and interview a few photographers. Show the photographer ads that interest you. Clearly explain the look and concept of the shots you want.

A photographer told me about a singer who was doing a shot for her album cover. The singer wanted a tough sexy look but did not make that clear to the photographer. Although the photographer made her look beautiful, the singer was unhappy with the photographs. Make sure the photographer really understands what you need.

Things to Consider When Choosing a Photographer

Notice how the photographer responds to your photo selections. Does the photographer have recommendations for other types of shots?

Will the photographer shoot on location? "On location" means shooting your photos outside the photographer's studio—for instance, at an airport, bank, in your home, at the ocean or at a ski resort. Try to shoot a few of your "ads" in interesting locations. Ask around and see if you have access to a doctor's office, court room, gym, computer store, garage, library, school, or restaurant. You might be surprised how helpful people can be when you approach them nicely, and clearly explain to them that you are trying to put together shots for your composite sheet or portfolio. Make sure they understand that you are not producing an ad.

Normally, people are paid to have their facility used for an ad, or at least get a name credit in the ad. When shooting on location, make sure the person who is giving you permission to shoot knows exactly what the shot will look like. You do not want to run into a situation where the owner of a store doesn't feel comfortable with the type of shot you are doing, and asks you to leave in the middle of the session. Clearly explain the type of shot, the approximate length of the session, and how many people will be involved. Ask when it would be most convenient for them. Don't disrupt any business that might be going on while you are shooting.

Leave the place looking even better than before you got there. Don't burn any bridges; you might want to go back there again at some point. Send a thank you note, and definitely send a copy of the shot and/or your composite sheet with the photo on it as a way of saying thanks.

With the photographer's permission, you can offer to let the establishment use your photo in an ad at no charge. If your shot won't work as an ad for the establishment, perhaps the photographer would agree to do one free publicity photo for the business. If the photographer is just getting started, doing a free photo could be a good way to make a contact with the business owner and add to his or her portfolio. Make sure the shots can be done, both technically and within your budget.

Do you feel comfortable with the photographer? This is just as important as the quality of the photographer's work. You must be able to relax and try out ideas during a shoot, otherwise the camera will capture your anxiety, and your photos will show you looking uncomfortable. View the photographer's portfolio. See if he or she has taken any photos in the same style you desire. If not, you should not necessarily dismiss the photographer. Perhaps the photographer can do a wonderful job, but has not had the opportunity to shoot in that particular style. The main thing to look for is the clarity and "life" in the shots. Are they in focus? Do the models look sharp, and show personality? A sign of a good photo is that when you initially look at the picture you immediately are attracted to the model's eyes. If the photos look clear but are not especially creative, don't worry. Remember, you are the one who will be bringing many ideas to the shot.

Before hiring a photographer to shoot your photos, make sure you get the following information:

What are the fees?

You can expect to pay anywhere from $100 to $800 for the session. Fees vary depending on the package offered, types of shots, and the location of the studio.

Does the fee include a makeup artist, or does the model have to pay for one?

The cost for a professional makeup artist can range from $40 to $200. The average fee in large markets is $100. For a discussion on whether you'll need a makeup artist, see the section "Hire a Makeup Artist" later in this chapter.

Should you use black-and-white or color?

Years ago everyone began with black-and-white comps, because color was too expensive. Due to the advanced technology and reduced costs of the laser and Indigo process (see "Glossary of Terms") color comps are now affordable. For a printed comp, use black-and-white photos. For small quantities of laser or Indigo comps, color photos can be used. One thousand copies of a high-quality all-color composite sheet could cost anywhere from $700 to $1800. Black-and-white comps could cost from $100 to $600.

How many rolls of film will be used?

A minimum of two rolls with fifteen shots for each image should be enough.

Will he or she shoot Polaroids?

Polaroids are pictures that develop in less than a minute, so that you can quickly see how the shot looks. Polaroids can give you an idea of what the final shot will look like, so that you can make last-minute changes or adjustments. They are not used for your comp.

How many 8 x 10 photos will you receive?

The standard size photo given to the model from the session is 8 x 10. What are the fees for additional 8 x 10 prints?

Can you keep the negatives?

Legally, the negatives belong to the photographer. However, it is always better to have the negatives in your possession. Many photographers will not give them up, but it's worth asking. If you have the negatives and you need more photos immediately, you do not have to wait for the photographer who did your comp shots to make up the prints. Keeping the negatives also means there are fewer chances that unauthorized shots of you will ever appear.

How long will it take to print the contact sheets?

A contact sheet shows in miniature size all the photos taken at the session. It is from the contact sheet that you will choose the photos you want. Here is what a contact sheet looks like.

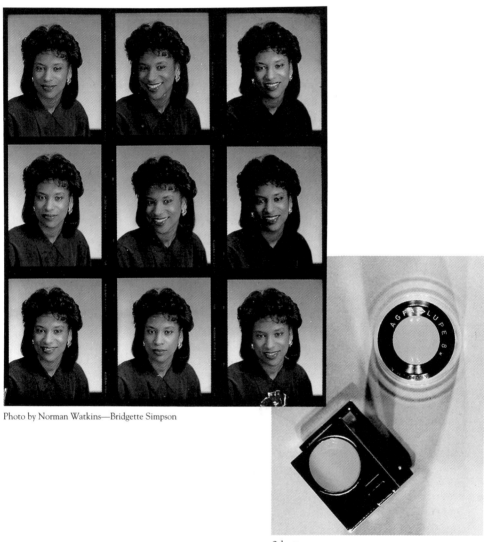

Photo by Norman Watkins—Bridgette Simpson

2 loupes

Don't worry about whether the photos on the contact sheet look a bit too light or dark; the lighting can be drastically changed when a final print is made. Choose your photos based on your expression and the focus of the shot. The best way to view them is with a loupe, which is a magnifying device that helps you see the photos on the contact sheet in great detail.

Will a fee be charged if you are not happy with the photos and need to reshoot?

Most photographers will tell you that as long as they did not make any technical mistakes — such as poor focus or lighting — they will charge the full fee to reshoot. Still, you should always ask because I have heard of some photographers either offering to reshoot at no charge or for a discount if the model is not happy with the photos.

Tips for Dealing with Photographers' Fees

You should request (not demand) to pay a percentage of the photographer's fee up front, then pay the balance when everything that was agreed to is completed. Many photographers expect to be paid in full the day of the session. Just keep in mind that you always have a better chance of getting all of your photos delivered to you on time if the photographer has not been paid in full.

Try to get all agreements in writing and signed by the photographer. The agreement can be written in plain English. This is not a common practice, but is worth trying.

Hiring a Makeup Artist

You might wonder: "Do I really need to pay the extra money for a makeup artist? I could do the makeup myself." But, even if you are great at doing your own makeup, there is a big difference between the way makeup is applied for personal use and for the camera. However, as I'll explain in the next chapter, it is also important for models to learn how to apply their own makeup. Professional makeup artists know what the camera needs. They will also stay with you during the shoot, and fix any hairs that have fallen out of place, and powder your face if it gets shiny under the lights.

Makeup artists can help in other ways too. I recently had a photo session for a new head shot. Even though I know how to do may own makeup, I hired a professional makeup artist. Not only did my face look better, but she noticed in the Polaroids that I was leaning towards the camera slightly and was not sitting straight. This caused my head to look extremely thin and almost detached from my body. This slight adjustment made a big difference. Sometimes photographers can help spot problems while shooting, but they are concentrating on other aspects of the shot.

Erasing mistakes, such as hairs out of place and lint on clothes, can be performed with computer programs such as Photoshop, but it is a very expensive procedure and should only be used as a last resort to save a picture that you really need. It is usually cheaper to pay a makeup artist than it is to try to get photos retouched after the session.

Sometimes the makeup artist can also serve as a "stylist." A stylist selects the clothing or "wardrobe" and props for the shoot. For shoots with a large budget, a makeup artist is hired strictly to do makeup, and a stylist is hired to coordinate and purchase the wardrobe. Discuss the shots with the makeup artist before the session. Show the makeup artist all the sample shots you will be doing. It is just as important for the makeup artist to understand the concept and feel of the shots as the photographer. If the makeup artist is also helping with styling—wardrobe and props—ask if any special props or clothing are needed. If so, make a list of them.

If you have a unique skin tone and use special makeup, or can only use certain makeup because of allergies, always bring the makeup to your sessions. The makeup artist will apply it for you. Make sure you tell the makeup artist if you will be wearing contact lenses. He or she will be extra careful when applying makeup around your eyes.

Don't allow your skin to burn in the sun. Sunburn is never good for you, but especially not before a photo session. A young girl I know sat out in the sun for many hours just days before getting photos done for her composite sheet. When she got her pictures back she noticed that her skin actually looked orange and red.

Before the Session

Make sure an iron is on the set, even if you have to bring your own. Wrinkled clothing makes a shot look unprofessional. Unless the clothes should be wrinkled to achieve a particular look, always have the wardrobe look neat and clean. Everything should be planned ahead of time so there are no major surprises on the day of the shoot.

After checking everything on your list, iron and hang all the wardrobe in a garment bag the night before a morning session. Place all props in a bag. Make sure you get a good night's sleep. Go over the list one more time in the morning. One of my very first jobs was working as an extra on a TV series. I was hired to be a waiter. I was so excited that I threw my wardrobe together that morning and went rushing off to the job. When I arrived on the set (which was a hotel in Washington D.C.) I suddenly realized that I had forgotten to bring a very important part of my wardrobe: black pants. Fortunately I arrived twenty-five minutes before my call time. I literally begged every person connected with the hotel to lend me a pair of black pants. The few people who were kind enough to offer their trousers had waists that were either way too large or too small. I ran across the street to another hotel and paid a waiter just about everything I was earning that day to borrow his pants for the day. Since then, I always go over my wardrobe list before leaving for a shoot.

Give yourself plenty of time to get to your session. Do not bring friends or relatives to the shoot. You don't want to be distracted by having your friends watch your session. This is a time you need to concentrate. Of course, this rule does not apply to the adult who brings a child model to a photo session. Sometimes the adult is asked to be present on the set to help the child relax, but other times the adult can be distracting and might be asked to wait in another room during the shoot. Once on the set, try to relax and enjoy the session. You will learn what to do on the set in the "Go-See" section of Chapter 8.

After the Session

Study the contact sheets. Ask other people in the industry for their opinion. If you haven't already, now would be a good time to begin contacting agents. Have them look at the contact sheets. See if any photos jump off the page. Before selecting the shots for your comp, make sure you really like them. Your pictures are representing you. In some cases you only get one chance to meet with an agent, art director, or photographer. Do not waste a good opportunity by showing poor-quality photographs. If the shots did not work, do not use them. Try to figure out what went wrong and shoot them again.

For my acting work I once used a head shot that broke all of the rules for head shots (see photo number 1 on next page). Instead of a nice warm smile, the shot had a "character" look: I have a quirky smile. My hand is on my chin. Half of my face is dark. It worked very well for me; I would land the sleazy salesman, crazy scientist, or nerd-type roles. Although my agents knew I could do other roles, it was hard for them to submit me for straighter castings, because the producers and casting directors would look at my head shot and immediately think of me as a character actor only. Models, like actors, can get "type cast" and only get certain kinds of roles. Fortunately, models have the opportunity to show a number of different looks on their composite sheet.

To make myself more presentable for the "straighter" roles I decided to have a new head shot taken. I worked very hard at preparing for my session. I spent countless hours trying to figure out how I wanted to present myself. I wanted to change the "character" look that I had been known for. I found a head shot in an agent's book that I loved (see photo number 2 on next page). The model was almost expressionless. The lighting was dark and serious. I thought that type of look would give me the opportunity to audition for more significant parts. It was exactly what I was looking for.

I did the session. The photographer did everything I asked. The lighting was perfect. I took the contact sheets around to some agents. They all said the same thing: "Aaron, you look dead. I don't see any life in your face. I can't tell what type of person you are from this photo." I saw what they were talking about. I had done a 180 degree turn with my head shot. I went from a real character look to a completely blank look. The photo did not express my personality. I had to go back to the drawing board and figure out what changes were needed in order for my head shot to reveal my personality.

Try this exercise when you are deciding on the image for your head shot. When you talk to people who do not know you very well ask them how you are perceived. This is what happens when you walk into a casting office. Before you even say hello, the casting agent has already decided if you will be considered for the part. Everyone has a certain presence, and that is what you want to capture on your head shot. I asked people in and out of the business (who did not know much about me) how they viewed me. Nice guy, friendly, honest, warm, smart, were some of the descriptions I would repeatedly hear. After learning that information I knew what kind of feeling and image I wanted to project for my head shot (see photo number 3 below).

1. Photo by Allen Polansky

2. Photo by Norman Watkins

3. © Fred Sons

The point is, just because you do a session, don't think that you will always get exactly what you need. Be prepared to go back and do things again. Maybe the expressions you wanted were not there. Perhaps the wardrobe did not quite fit the image desired. You might not have been able to relax during the session. Some photos do not work because of the photographer: the lighting is bad, the picture is out of focus or the camera angle is not complimentary to your face. If you like the way you look but not the overall photo, then you might need to find a new photographer. It is better to wait, figure out what is wrong, and try it again. It happens to everyone.

After choosing the photos for your comp, make sure you have at least two copies of each photo you want to use. If you can afford it, get three or four. You always want extra copies in case something happens to the original. Some photographs are irreplaceable.

One quick comment about the photographer's name or photo credit. Some models put the photographer's name by the side of the photo on composite sheets. This is a courtesy to the photographer, but is not necessary. If all of your shots were taken by one photographer you might not want to list the photographer's name, because it will immediately show your lack of experience. If you have appeared in a lot of ads, you will have worked with many photographers, and can list many different photographers' names. It is your choice, but one name on all the photos is a dead giveaway of inexperience.

Designing and Printing Your Composite Sheet

If small quantities are all you need, laser printing is a less expensive alternative to offset printing. Offset printing is how most composite sheets are made. It is a process of transferring the images of the photographs onto paper.

Reproducing 100 black-and-white laser could cost as little as $40. Ask your agent if he or she will accept laser comps before getting any printed.

If it's not your first comp, the question of whether to use color or black-and-white is an esthetic and financial decision. Some photos look better in black-and-white and some look better in color. If you have certain features that you want to show, like red hair, the only way it can be noticed is by having the shot in color.

You must decide how much of an investment you want to make. One job could pay for all of your comps. You have to spend money in order to produce a great composite sheet. If you are not willing to make the investment, you are not giving yourself a chance to see what you can do in this industry.

A graphic artist can get the comp "camera ready" for the printer. That means all the graphic work is completed and the comp is ready to be photographed and printed.

Some printers will do the graphics for you. There may be additional fees if the printer's graphic artist designs your comp. If you are not using a standard layout offered by the company, then you need to provide a detailed mock-up (design) that clearly shows how you want the photos placed.

Some companies specialize in composite sheet and head shot reproduction. *The Marcus Institute's Industry Information Directory* lists companies located in the United States and Canada who perform this work. See Chapter 12: "Resources."

Before deciding on a company, make sure you see samples of their work. Most companies will send them to you. Find out if your material must be camera ready or if the printer will take care of the graphic work. Ask how long will it take to complete your job. Clearly understand all the costs involved. Ask about the price, and how much it will cost to reorder more copies.

If you are having an out-of-town company reproduce your comps, ask what the fee would be for you to have a sample of your composite sheet faxed or mailed to you before it is printed. Making sure that everything on the composite sheet is exactly how you want it would be well worth a small fee.

When mailing photos to a duplicating company or printer, always send the original photographs. This will give you the sharpest and clearest image.

Do not touch the photos with your fingers, because you do not want fingerprints on the image. Keep them clean and scratch free. Keep them away from sun and heat, which can damage your photos. Put your name and phone number on the back corner of the photographs. Never place it directly behind your face or anywhere where it could be seen on the actual image. It is better to use a self-stick label than to write on the back of a photo. If you need to write on the back of a photo, use a smear-proof pen so your name and phone number will stay clear and readable. This will make your photo identifiable in case it gets separated from the package. To keep your photos from bending, sandwich them between strong pieces of cardboard. Place them in an envelope that has the words "photographs—do not bend" on the front and back.

How many comps should you order?

It depends on your situation. If you are just starting in the business and working with one agent, 200 comps should be plenty. If you are working with a number of agents, make sure you get enough comps to provide each agent with as many as he or she needs until you are ready to produce a new composite sheet. Keep in mind that you will have to periodically resupply your agents with comps as they run out.

When you first get your comps from the printer, save a few dozen in a special place for emergencies. You never want to tell a person requesting a comp that you just ran out. It looks unprofessional and you could lose a lot of money if it costs you a job. Order more when you see that you are low on comps.

Get quotes for ordering different amounts. You might be surprised how little difference there is between ordering 200 and 500 comps or even 1000 and 2000 comps. One of the big costs with composite sheets is the printer's setup time. Once a printer begins printing, you are only paying for extra paper.

The Ingredients of a Professional Composite Sheet

All comps should include:

1. Photos

2. Information about your size and appearance:

For a woman:	**For a man:**
height	height
bust	suit size
waist	neck/sleeve
hips	waist
dress size	inseam
shoes	shoes
eye color	eye color
hair color	hair color
hat size	hat size
glove size	glove size
ring size	ring size

3. Union affiliation—state whether you are a member of SAG, AFTRA, AEA, ACTRA, or The Models Guild.

4. Name, phone number (remember the area code) and fax number, if you have one.

5. Special qualities: for example, if appropriate, mention that you have excellent legs, hands, feet, or teeth.

6. Any sport or activity you are proficient in.

7. You may want to place the photographers' names on the comp, next to the photographs they took.

YOUR EYES WILL NOT BELIEVE THE RANGE OF AARON MARCUS!

HEIGHT: 6' 0"
SUIT: 39L
NECK/SLEEVE: 15 34/35
WAIST: 33
INSEAM: 32
SHOE: 10

HAIR: LT. BROWN
EYES: BLUE
SAG/AFTRA
GOOD HANDS
PROFESSIONAL GUITARIST
ALL SPORTS

AARON MARCUS

Expressions ™

MODELING & TALENT AGENCY, INC.
104 Church Street, Philadelphia, PA 19106
Phone: (215) 923-4420 • Fax: (215) 440-7179

↑   *Stats on the composite*   ↑

Composite Sheets for Children

If you are interested in getting your child or children in the business, you are probably wondering if a composite sheet or head shot is really needed. The best thing to do is ask the manager or agent with whom you are working or want to work with, and find out how they want to submit your child's photo. Everyone has different policies. Many agents require only a snapshot of a child under the age of three, since their looks change so quickly. A photo that is three months old might not properly represent the child's current appearance. After the age of four (depending on how quickly the child's look changes), most agents will request a head shot. A composite sheet is only used when a child has very different and distinctive looks, and might not be needed until the child is at least seven to ten years old.

6

Makeup

Both men and women should learn how to apply their own makeup. At the very least, all models should know how to put on base and powder. Most faces have slightly uneven shades of lightness and darkness. Putting on a base will smooth, darken, and even your skin tone. Imagine the base as a canvas for a painting. Once the base is applied you can begin "painting," by applying other makeup on top of the base. The base will help cover up slight imperfections, and if needed will hide a five o'clock shadow. The powder helps take the shine off your face. This is extremely important when you are working under hot lights.

For many jobs, models are expected to do their own makeup. The better you are at putting on makeup, the better you will look in the shot. This skill will also help you at go-sees. You can cover up circles under your eyes, dry skin, or blemishes before a Polaroid is taken.

I had a go-see in February. The character was supposed to live in California, and spend a lot of time outside in the sun. I did not have much of a tan, but because I know how to apply makeup, I was able to put foundation over my hands, face, neck, and ears and rouge on my cheeks to give me a sunburned, outdoorsy look. I really looked the part. Knowing how to apply makeup gives you a great advantage at go-sees.

When you work with a professional makeup artist, ask about the best products and tones for your face. If possible, ask for a basic demonstration of how to apply makeup. Watch the artist work on other models. Perhaps there is a school in your area that teaches makeup application. If you do not have contact with a professional makeup person, go to a cosmetic store and speak to a professional about products and application used for modeling. If you have a unique skin tone and use special makeup, always bring it to the set even if a makeup artist has been hired.

■ ■ ■ ■ ■

1. Makeup for Women
This is a basic list of makeup needed by women:

- Good foundation
- Facial cleaner
- Toner
- Skin lotion
- Nail polish (neutral colors)
- Nail polish remover
- Hair spray
- Translucent powder
- Light blush
- Brown eye shadow
- Black mascara
- Matte lipstick
- Concealer for around eyes

2. Makeup For Men
This is a basic list of makeup needed by men:

- Base or foundation
- Vaseline (for lips)
- Blush
- Concealer for around eyes
- Hair spray
- Razor and shaving cream
- Skin Lotion
- Translucent powder
- Gel for hair

3. Additional items to bring to a shoot:
You probably won't need to bring all of these items. Pick and choose the ones that are most relevant for you.

- Comb
- Small towel
- Head bands
- Bobby pins
- Eye drops
- Small first aid kit
- Compact mirror
- Lint brush
- Ziploc bags for small items that could spill
- Toothbrush/toothpaste/dental floss/mouthwash
- If appropriate, extra stockings: white, black and blue
- Money for parking and food
- Change for phone calls and parking meters
- Map of the area where you are working
- Pen
- Vouchers
- Calculator for filling out your voucher
- Small emergency sewing kit/safety pins/extra buttons
- Brush
- Cotton swabs—Cotton Balls
- Pony tail rubber bands
- Nail clippers/emery boards
- Aspirin
- Deodorant
- Shampoo
- Light snack (non-perishable)
- Extra composite sheets
- Mini book (small book showing your photos)
- Reading material
- Small calendar book to remind you when to contact people, or for names, addresses and information

7

Finding A Good Agent

An agent's job is to submit your composite sheet to art directors and photographers, give you the necessary information pertaining to a booking, negotiate and collect fees when you are booked for a job, and to send you on go-sees. Photographers, art directors, and the clients select models for jobs. All you can ask of your agent is to be submitted. An agent who has worked with a photographer or art director for many years might be asked to suggest or recommend a specific model. If the photographer or art director agrees with the suggestion, then that model will get top priority and have their card shown to the client or requested at the go-see. The agent does not select models for jobs.

Quite often there is no way to know why one gets cast. Sometimes, the casting process seems entirely arbitrary. For example, I was once cast as a construction worker. I was very surprised because I do not see myself as having the construction worker look. After the shoot I asked the casting director why I got the job. He told me that at every construction site there is always one person who looks like he does not belong there. So, oddly enough, I got booked because I did not look right for the part.

Fees for Agents

Agents who specialize in print advertising charge anywhere from 10 to 20 percent commission per booking. If you have an exclusive contract with an agent, you might be responsible for paying your agent a percentage of all of your bookings, including those you get on your own. Travel reimbursement (train or plane fare) is separate from the hourly fee and is not subject to commission.

Sometimes models get paid for the time they spend traveling to a job, when the shoot is in a distant location. Agents will take a commission from that fee.

Agents collect a fee only when they obtain a booking for a model. The only exception to this rule is when a model decides to be in an agent's book or poster. I will discuss agents' books and posters in Chapter 8: "How to Get Work."

■ ■ ■ ■ ■

Listings of Agents

There are many ways to find an agent. Some are very traditional methods; others require using your creativity and ingenuity. A simple way of finding an agent is to purchase a list or a directory of agents in the area where you want to be represented. The list can be obtained through companies that handle modeling information and products. The Models Mart, 1-800-223-1254, sells modeling books, directories, and lists of agents. Their *International Directory of Model and Talent Agencies & Schools* can help you find agents in your community, and in other markets. *Ross Reports*, 212-536-5170, is a monthly booklet that lists many New York and Los Angeles casting directors, franchised talent agents and literary agents. *Ross Reports* is primarily used by actors, but some actors' agents also represent commercial models.

The *Madison Avenue Handbook*, also known as *The Image Makers Source*, lists agents and New York advertising agencies, but its primary value is in the additional information it offers on the production of shoots—equipment rental, music, sound, film and tape production, lighting, set design and car rental companies.

Contacting Agents

By using the *Marcus Institute's National Directory of SAG and AFTRA Offices* (for more information about this directory, see Chapter 12: "Resources.") you can call your nearest office and ask them to mail or fax you a **free** list of franchised agents who are signatories with SAG and AFTRA. These agents have signed contracts with SAG and AFTRA agreeing to honor and abide by many rules and regulations. Most of these franchised agents also have a commercial modeling division along with their TV and radio department. One quick phone call can give you a great start or advancement in finding a good agent.

There is no guarantee that these agents are wonderful and trustworthy, but you will have a much better chance of finding good representation with franchised agents than by picking names blindly out of a large directory.

Many agents listed in *Ross Reports* request no phone calls. Honor that request. If the agent allows calls, ask when the agent has "open call." Open call is when an agent allows new people to come to his or her office and introduce themselves. If calling is not appropriate, send in a composite sheet. If you only have a head shot, send the head shot and briefly describe your modeling experiences. Make sure your phone number is on your comp and cover letter, so the agent knows how to contact you. When sending a package to an agency you should always try to address it to a specific person. Call the agency if you do not have a name. Do not address it "To Whom It May Concern." Your package will be viewed much more favorably when sent with the agent's name on the envelope and on your cover letter. This applies to all mailings.

When I first wanted to get into the business I did not know the names of any agents. Nor did I know about any lists of agents that were available. I had to be creative. First, I attended a number of plays, and talked to the actors afterward. I asked them for the names and numbers of their agents, and whether those agents worked with commercial models. I contacted a local advertising association to get the names of the largest advertising agencies in the area. I called a few art directors and asked them which agents they use when booking models for ads. I even went through the phone book to get names of photographers to find out who they use for booking models. (Asking agents about photographers is also a good way of compiling a list of photographers to interview.)

In some areas, it can be very difficult to find an agent. An actor I know was looking for a New York agent. He sent out his head shot, copies of awards and reviews from plays he had appeared in (which included a wonderful review in *The New York Times*). He mailed his package to 160 agents, but received only one response. However, that agent signed him, and he has landed some wonderful film and TV roles. For print work as well as TV and film, you only need one great agent for your career to take off.

After contacting the agent, make sure you follow the agent's rules and policies. Once I was in an agent's office that had a sign on the door that clearly said "by appointment only." A model walked in asking for one of the bookers by name. (A booker is someone who contacts the models for go-sees and makes booking arrangements. There could be up to seven or eight bookers working at one modeling agency.) The model told the booker that he had spoken with her a few months ago and wanted to drop off some of his composite sheets and set up an appointment to show her his mini book (a small book that contains the model's portfolio). The booker told the model that "the agency won't be interviewing new models for another six months." After the model left the booker threw all of the model's comps into the trash can. I was stunned. I saw the comps, and they looked very good. I asked why she threw them away. She said, "If the model does not have the courtesy to follow our basic rule of not coming into the office without an appointment, how could we trust him to act responsibly on a shoot when he would be representing our agency?" By not following one of the agency's primary policies, this model lost the opportunity to be represented by a great agency. Different agents have different ways of running their agency. It is important to respect their wishes.

Make Sure the Agent is Legitimate

Most agents are honest and hard-working people, but there are a few scam artists out there that you should be aware of.

There are some people who call themselves agents but actually make their living ripping off models. They prey on people who make decisions based on their emotions instead of good sound judgment. Often, they will tell you that you have a lot of potential, and that with their guidance they will make you a star. They might ask for up-front money to cover their promotional expenses. If that happens, walk out the door.

Legitimate agents make their money by getting a percentage of the bookings they get for the model. Corrupt agents make money not by booking models, but by receiving "up-front money," and by sending models to a photographer who actually works for them. The model will be told that all of his or her head shots and composite sheets must be shot by this one photographer. They will charge extraordinary fees for the work.

A few years ago I saw an ad in a Washington D.C. paper from a "New York" agent who was relocating and looking for models. It felt like a scam to me, and I wanted to see first hand how these thieves operate. I called and set up an interview with the "agent." I pretended that I had no experience and told him that I wanted to be a model. He told me that he rates everyone on a scale of one to five. If I was a five he would represent me. He told me I was a four. I told him how disappointed I was and began to leave. I knew he was not going to let me walk out the door. As I put my hand on the door knob he said, "Aaron, you know what, you are a four but you are very close to being a five. In fact I know a great photographer who could turn you into a five. With the right pictures I could start sending you up to New York." What he failed to mention was that the "great" photographer was part of his company. I should have gotten an Academy Award for the excitement I showed when I found out that I could become a five and be sent to New York. I told him that I had never been professionally photographed, still he was promising to send me to New York. No credible agent would risk their reputation by sending someone with no experience to the largest commercial modeling market in the world. I asked the agent, "What do I do next?" He whipped out a contract and said "All you have to do is sign here." I very quickly glanced at the contract and noticed the cost of the photo was $1,200. I told him I definitely wanted to do this but I would have to look the contract over at home and come back the next day. He put his hand on the contract and told me that "the contract does not leave his office." He also said that "a model's and agent's relationship is built on trust. If you can't trust your agent then your agent will not be able to get work for you." I told him that I would have to call him back, and left. This guy was a sophisticated and manipulative con man.

To help you choose a reputable agent, I have put together a list of things to look for when interviewing with an unfamiliar agent:

- Make sure your appointment is scheduled during work hours.
- Always meet the agent at his or her office. Do not meet with an unfamiliar agent anywhere else.

- Look around the office. Are there pictures of ads they have booked for their models? If so, this is a good sign.
- Are the phones ringing? You want to see a busy office.
- Ask to see the head shots and comps of the models they represent. Do they look good? You might want to request to see the comps of a few of the models whose ads are displayed in the office. These charlatans have been known to fool people by placing ads in their office of models they do not represent. If an agent is really working with a model he or she should have the model's composite sheet on hand.
- Ask to see their agency poster or book (photos of models they represent). Have you seen these models in any ads?
- If you know any models who work with the agent, call them before your interview. Do they like the agent? Do they get work through the agent? Does the agent treat them well? Are they paid on time? (Generally payments are made within 90 days.)
- Do you feel comfortable with the agent?
- Call the local SAG, AFTRA, or ACTRA office. They have nothing to do with commercial modeling, but they might have some information about the agency.
- Call The Models Guild or the Better Business Bureau to see if any complaints have been made against the agency.
- If the agent lies to you, makes outrageous promises, or asks for money (to cover phone calls or mailing expenses on your behalf), keep looking. Legitimate agents do not ask for expense money.

Signing With an Agent

Some commercial modeling agents ask models to sign exclusive contracts. If you sign an exclusive contract, you may only accept bookings from that agent. You may, however, be able to accept a booking with another agent if you obtain permission from your agent. If you are not signed with an agent, you can freelance and accept bookings from any agent.

There are pros and cons to signing with an agent. On the positive side, you will have one person working very hard on your behalf. You will only need to supply one agent with composite sheets, mini books, and head shots. Life is simpler. When you are not available to work on certain days, you only need to notify one agent.

On the negative side, some models sign contracts with agents who can't or won't get them work. I met a model on a shoot who was signed by a large New York agency. Let's call the model Tom. The agent had no intention of sending Tom out on go-sees. They signed him because they feared if Tom signed with another agency, he could take away business from their own signed models. Tom was given a contract for the sole purpose of not allowing him to compete with the agent's signed models.

If you are just beginning, don't sign long-term agreements with an agent you are unfamiliar with. If asked to sign, find out how many other models in your "category" are already signed. Your "category" includes other models who could be booked for the same job as you. There will always be other signed models in your category. However, it is not in your best interest to be one of 50 others who could be submitted for the same job. If yours is the only agent sending models to a go-see, you have a much better chance of getting booked for the job if there are fewer models in your category. See if you can work out a trial period of three to six months. If you like the way you are being represented, sign a longer-term contract.

Before signing with an agent, make sure you understand everything in the contract. If you are not sure about something, show it to a lawyer. Be careful out there.

Getting an Agent's Attention

If you want to be represented by a particular agent, but you are having a difficult time making a connection, here is something you can try. Book a job on your own, and ask the agent if he or she will handle the booking. Chances are the agent will be glad to represent you. It will be easily made money for the agent. The small percentage that you will lose will be well worth the connection you will have made. The first time I gave a booking to an agent I actually made money, because the agent negotiated a much higher fee than I could have.

8

How To Get Work

The best way to get work is to find an agent, or agents, who will submit your composite sheet and send you out on go-sees.

Agency Books and Posters

Many agencies publish talent books and/or posters. The only fees agents collect from models, aside from a percentage of the model's bookings, is a fee to appear on the agent's poster or in their book. Being shown on the poster or in the book can cost anywhere from $30 to $700. Fees vary depending on the format (color or black-and-white photos), whether you pay for a whole, half, or quarter of a page, and the location of the agency. This promotional tool gets sent to photographers and advertising agencies. Many models get jobs directly from the book or poster without attending a go-see. It is difficult for an agent to promote a model who isn't willing to be in the agent's book or on the poster.

There is no guarantee of getting work, but having great photos for your comps, agency books, and posters will greatly increase your chances of working (see examples on next page).

■ ■ ■ ■ ■

Women's poster—McDonald/Richards Model Management, Inc.

Page from McDonald/Richards Model Management, Inc. book

Selling Yourself

Some people think that once an agency begins submitting their comp, all they need to do is wait by the phone. This is a dangerous way to run a business. You will get more work if you work at selling yourself. Try to mail comps to as many photographers and art directors as possible. This will give you greater exposure to more people.

To help find contacts refer to the *Standard Directory of Advertisers* and the *Directory of Advertising Agencies*. These incredible resource materials are published annually, and can be found at many libraries. They are both commonly referred to as the *Agency Red Book*. The *Standard Directory of Advertisers* lists basic information about many companies, including the types of products or services they offer, and the name, address, and phone number of the advertising agency or agencies that produce their ads. If you feel you have the look for, let's say, a beer, sports car, or computer ad, look up the companies in the *Standard Directory of Advertisers* and find out who does their advertising.

The Directory of Advertising Agencies offers information about ad agencies and their clients. This book will give you the names of the advertising agencies in your state. Send your composite sheet to the ad agencies, to the attention of the art or creative director. The creative director generally creates the concept of the ad and oversees and approves the project. As I mentioned in Chapter 7: "Finding a Good Agent," *The Madison Avenue Handbook* lists many New York advertising agencies. This Peter Glenn publication can be found at libraries, or it can be purchased through The Models Mart for around $50.

It's also helpful to send notes, post cards, or new comps to photographers you have already worked with. This reminds them that you are still available for work. Some photographers will tell you it is a waste of time to send comps to them, because when they are ready to cast for a job they will look through agents' books and have a go-see. Yet I have gotten a number of jobs from photographers I had just sent a new comp or note to. I do not believe it was a coincidence. There is a photographer who I had never worked for, but I had heard good things about his work. Every time I put a new composite sheet together I send him one. This has been going on for three years. I never heard a word from him. Then one day, out of the clear blue, I got a phone call from his studio. He wanted to book me for a job. When I met him on the set he told me that he always loved my comps, but never had a project that I was right for.

It is always helpful to keep your name and face in front of as many people as possible. After sending out comps, wait about a week and make a follow-up phone call. Just ask if your composite sheet arrived. You don't have to get through to the photographer; you do not want to interrupt a photo session to ask about your comp. Perhaps the office manager or assistant can tell you if your comp has arrived safe and sound.

Some photographers and art directors will agree to meet or talk with models over the phone. The best policy is to call and ask. If they will meet with you, bring a mini book, or portfolio, and some comps.

If you want to be represented in different markets, having a Polaroid camera can be very helpful. If you live in Miami and want to be considered for bookings in Chicago, you can't easily fly to Chicago, even for a request go-see (that is when a client specifically asks for a certain model to "audition"). Since the photographer and client will want to see what you currently look like, you can take a Polaroid in your home and send it by overnight mail.

If you are working with one agent or feel your phone number could change in the near future, list your agent's name and number your comp. That way, you will always be reachable. Models who can't be reached will not work. If you are working with a few agents or plan to market yourself, have your phone number, including the area code, on your comp. Most agents will put their own labels over your phone number when submitting your comp to a client. Since you never know who will get your comp, you may prefer not to have your home phone number listed. Instead use an answering service or a number that only goes to an answering machine or voice mail.

Staying in Touch with Your Agent

You must have an answering machine, beeper, or a phone service. Agents will not try to get you work if they can't reach you.

Keep your outgoing message less than twenty-five seconds. Your agent might need to call many people for a go-see. If your message is very long, the agent might hang up and call someone else.

Check your machine at least three times a day. After receiving a call about a booking or go-see, call the agent back as soon as possible, even if it's to let him or her know you can't accept the job or attend the go-see. Sometimes an agent only has a limited amount of people that he or she can send to a go-see. If you are not free, give the agent an opportunity to send someone else. When agents spend large amounts of time trying to track down models, that leaves them less time to promote the models. If you have an answering machine make sure your message is short and to the point. Agents do not want to spend a lot of time sitting through a long message.

Always make sure your agent has enough composite sheets. If he or she runs out, your comp cannot be included in packages sent to clients, and you cannot be considered for a job. Sometimes agents will call to let you know that they need more comps, but ultimately it is your responsibility to make sure your agent has a good supply of comps. Give the agents as many comps as they request and periodically ask if more comps are needed. Sometimes it is hard to hear that your agent needs more comps because you will need to have more printed, but that also means that your agent is working to promote you.

Mini Books

When you have a reasonable number of pictures and tear sheets (copies of ads you appear in), you should begin putting together a "mini book." A mini book is a small book with plastic sleeves that holds about twenty 5 x 7 or 6 x 8 or 9 x 12 size photos. The mini book enables you to show photographers and clients more pictures than appear on your comp. Mini books are a necessity if you are interested in working in distant markets. You don't have to wait until you have enough photos to fill up an entire mini book before starting one. As you work, put more and more of your tear sheets in the book.

Some companies specialize in photographing tear sheets for mini books. Or, you may obtain laser copies of your ads, which is an inexpensive way to update your mini book on your own. A list of companies that sell mini books is also included free in the *Marcus Institute's Industry Information Directory*. See Chapter 12: "Resources."

Mini book

Working in Other Media

Although commercial modeling only involves print advertising, I recommend trying to work in as many media as possible: TV, film, radio, industrial films (training, instructional, or educational films for corporations and associations), along with print. All of these fields require the use of the same basic acting skills, so if work in one medium is slow, a different medium might be booming.

Go-See

What is a Go-See?

A go-see is an audition for print jobs such as magazine and newspaper ads. It generally takes place at a photographer's studio or casting office. After getting a call about a go-see, always ask your agent what character is being cast, so that you can look the part. Find out when the job will be shot. If you are not available, tell your agent. He or she may ask you to go anyway since shooting dates can change.

When you arrive, there should be a sign-in sheet and a model form to fill out. Models write their name and their agent's name on the sign-in sheet. This plain piece of paper lets everyone know who is next in line to have his or her Polaroid taken. Since you never know exactly when your name will be called off the list, do not sign in until you are completely—physically and mentally—ready to have your Polaroid taken.

SAMPLE MODEL FORM

(NAME OF PHOTOGRAPHER OR CASTING STUDIO)

DATE:

NAME: _____   PHONE: _____

AGENCY: _____   PHONE: _____

    HEIGHT: _____   SIZE: _____

    WAIST: _____   HIPS: _____

    SHIRT: _____   HAT: _____

    WEIGHT: _____   BUST: _____

    SHOES: _____   SUIT: _____

    INSEAM: _____   GLOVES: _____

    AGE: _____   HAIR: _____

    EYES: _____

ARE YOU AVAILABLE FOR TESTING? YES _____   NO _____

    THANK YOU

    STUDIO USE:

    COMMENTS ON MODEL!   POLAROIDS!

The model form asks for:

- Your name
- Agent's name
- Sizes
- Phone numbers, etc.

This information helps the stylist purchase the correct size clothing for the model selected for the job. It also lets the casting people know which agent to contact. Fill it out and hand it to the photographer or an assistant along with your composite sheet. Make sure your agent's name and phone number is on your comp.

You may choose not to write your home address on the model form. If you traveled to another city to attend a go-see, you might not want people to know that you live out-of-town. Sometimes that can keep a model from getting the booking, because some people are uncomfortable hiring out-of- town models. And, unless you have a P.O. Box number, it is wise to be selective about as to who gets your home address. If you are unsure about how to fill out the model form because of an out-of-town address, just ask your agent. You may want to get an 800 phone number. That takes care of the out-of-town issue, and prevents you from getting unwanted calls on your home phone number.

Layout

After filling out the model form, see if there is a layout. A layout is a vague image of the ad, which is used as a guide by the photographer, stylist and art director. It might give you specific information about the character being cast. You can see what the character looks like. Is the person wearing glasses? What are the attitudes and expressions?

At this point you should find a mirror in the makeup room or bathroom and try to make yourself look just like the character in the layout. Perhaps you need a little makeup or your hair needs to be combed again. You should also get yourself mentally prepared. Think of the message of the ad. What kind of emotions are being looked for? Think of the situations from your past or present that will allow you to actually feel the emotions needed for the shot. When you are ready, sign in. When it is your turn, a photographer or an assistant photographer will take the Polaroids.

Always ask what type of character is being looked for. Sometimes it is hard to fully understand the layout, or perhaps your interpretation of the ad might be different than the photographer's. Concepts can change and the layout may not represent

Layout—Shandwick U.S.A.

the real image wanted. The assistant photographer might not know much about the ad, but it's worth asking.

Right before the Polaroid is taken you will be asked to stand on a mark on the floor, (usually a piece of tape) or sit on a stool. Having everyone stand or sit in one spot means that the lighting can stay the same for everyone and makes focusing the camera easier for the photographer. Now is the time to use all of the techniques you have practiced. To help you concentrate on feeling the appropriate emotions, try looking at the floor or towards a wall. Once you feel the emotions look straight into the lens. If the layout shows the character looking away, look away. Try to copy the layout as closely as possible. If you need a moment to create that look, ask for it.

If you did not give the look you wanted, ask if they will take another Polaroid. Sometimes they say yes; sometimes they say no. I once went to a go-see for an ad for a new drug being given to cancer patients. I was supposed to look like a person with cancer. I tried to look sick, had the Polaroid taken and left. As I was getting on the elevator, it hit me that I gave a cold or flu kind of sick look, and not a more serious diseased expression. I felt a little uncomfortable but I went back and asked if I could try a different look. They said yes, and I got cast for the job. I might have gotten the job even if I didn't go back, but I felt much better knowing that I gave it my best try.

Photographers use Polaroids at go-sees so they can see what you currently look like and how closely you resemble the layout. Your composite sheet is viewed to see

Photo by Evan Cohen
Polaroid imitating layout from previous page

your range of looks. Normally the Polaroid will be attached to your comp and the model form. Sometimes regular 35mm film will be shot for the go-see and occasionally the go-see will be videotaped.

After your Polaroid is taken, wait around a few minutes to make sure the Polaroid looks okay. Sometimes the film or the lighting is bad and you will need to shoot it again. Ask if anyone is looking at mini books. Use your judgment. If it's a large casting and many people are waiting in line, it's doubtful that anyone will look at your book. See if the photographer wants a second composite sheet for his or her files. Sometimes the comp that you give a photographer is sent and kept by the art director or client. Make sure you always have extra comps with you.

A go-see should be viewed as a job. It is a good way to introduce yourself to a photographer and an art director. Never turn down a go-see. You never know how important one might be.

I once had an 8:00 a.m. audition in Washington, D.C. and a 12:30 p.m. go-see in New York. I rushed around like a mad man. There was a train delay and knew I would be late to the go-see. I called my agent and she suggested I still go. When I arrived about 20 minutes late, I realized why: There was a line that went down two flights of stairs, out the door and around the block. I waited in line for two hours. Some people decided to leave. But after all I had been through to get there, there was no way in the world I was going to walk out of line and go back home. I did have some doubts, though. There were a lot of beautiful men and women in line, and I wondered, "What in the world am I doing here? Does my agent have any idea what I look like?" I was feeling intimidated when I heard people talking about their latest movie roles, and their recent jobs on soaps. I finally made it upstairs, where the photographer was asking the models, on video tape, what they had done recently. Most people discussed their latest bookings. I knew the photographer must have been bored to death listening to hundreds of people talk about their latest jobs. I wanted to say something that was relevant to the shoot, but also have me stand out. Since this was an outdoors shot, I decided to tell him that what I did most recently was go on a camping trip with my family. As it turned out, among the hundreds and hundreds of people who attended the go-see, I got the booking, and was flown to Hawaii for the shoot.

I have gone to go-sees where I knew I was not right for the part and did not get the job. However, I was booked by the same photographer for a different job sometime later because the photographer remembered me.

There are a million reasons why people are and are not chosen for a job. Although it is difficult, try not to spend much time and energy wondering why you were not chosen. All you can do is give the look you are trying to achieve. The final results are out of your hands. If you did not achieve the look you wanted, try to figure out why.

Along with getting bookings, you should also use go-sees as an educational tool and a learning experience. They offer opportunities to introduce yourself to new people, and to remind people you have already worked with that you are still around.

How to Take a Better Polaroid

Some models show up to a go-see wearing anything they happen to fall into that particular day. They assume all photographers, casting agents and clients can use their imagination to see if you are right for the part. Don't count on it. You should look the part that is being cast. (This philosophy can change for certain acting auditions). Some casting directors feel insulted if you arrive at an audition wearing too much wardrobe. A good casting director can tell if you are right for the part purely by your acting skills. For go-sees, I prefer not to leave decisions up to people's imaginations. I like to hit them over the head with a look so they immediately think, "Yes, that person is perfect for the job."

If the client makes the final casting decision, then you are certainly better off dressing the part. Clients are not in the advertising business, and might not be able to see beyond the Polaroid. Even if the photographer, art director or casting person can envision someone looking a certain way, they may not be able or want to fight to get the model they want approved by the client. If they are looking for a business person, look like a business person.

You never know if they are going to take a close-up shot or a long shot of your whole body, so wear the whole suit, not a suit jacket and a pair of shorts.

Know your face. Be aware of which side of your face looks better on film. Once you have that information, you can always turn your face slightly towards the camera to show your best side. If your nose looks large in a profile shot (that means sideways), never turn completely sideways in front of the camera. You can "cheat to the camera" by turning your face a little towards the camera. This technique will make your nose look shorter. If possible, look at your Polaroid and the other models' Polaroids at a go-see. See what works and what doesn't. You can see how different your face can look by experimenting with different expressions and angles with a video or Polaroid camera.

Conflicts

After you appear in an ad for a certain product, all other competing products are considered conflicts. For example, Coke could be considered a conflict if your Pepsi ad is still running.

Before going to a go-see, ask your agent about the product. If there is a conflict, make sure your agent is aware of it. Sometimes casting agents tell the model's agent not to send anyone to the go-see who has done an ad for a competing product during the past year. Exclusivity fees are sometimes paid to the model so that the model will not work for a competitor. Once I did a job for a chain of hotels. For one year I could not do ads for hotels that were considered to be competitors. Before accepting other hotel jobs, my agent had to get permission from the advertising agency that paid me the exclusivity fee. If no exclusivity fee is paid, models may work for anyone who hires them. If there are any questions about a possible conflict, inform your agent.

Castings

A typical go-see in New York could easily draw 50 or more models auditioning for the same job. The selection process can be handled a number of different ways. Sometimes the photographer decides who gets cast for the job. Other times the photographer and/or art director will pick three or more people and list them as their first, second, and third choices. Phone calls go out to their agents to put the three models on hold. That means the models must hold the shooting date for that project. The model can't accept other bookings on that date without first clearing it with their agent. The first agent to put you on hold has the right of first refusal. That means if you get another job offering for the same date you are holding, you must have your agent call the photographer or art director who initially put you on hold, and have them either book you or release you. That allows the photographer or art director to hire you before anyone else for that date. You can only accept the second offer after being released from the first job.

Sometimes models are put on hold because a number of people—as many as seven or eight—might be involved in the casting process. Putting a number of people on hold gives everyone extra time to decide exactly who they want for the job. Sometimes it is the client who makes the final decision after getting input from the art director and/or photographer.

Information You'll Need After Accepting a Booking

- Date of the shoot
- Name and type of product
- Name and phone number of contact person
- Name of ad agency
- Name of the photographer
- Time and length of the shoot
- Location of and directions to the shoot

- Type of character desired
- Type of wardrobe needed
- Whether they will have a makeup artist on the set
- Billing and usage information (I will explain more about usage and billing later.)
- Fees

Agent Submittance

Another way to get booked, which does not involve a go-see, is through agent submittance. An ad agency or photographer might call an agent and request a specific look. The agent will submit a package of composite sheets of models who fit that description. There are new services currently available that allow agents to show models' photos on the Internet, and through other computer devices. These methods allow agents to show photographers and art directors the models they represent without having to mail composite sheets. Unlike a composite sheet, these photos can be easily updated.

Agents' Books and Posters

Another way of getting booked for a job is from the agent's book or poster sheet. Because of the expense and time involved in holding casting sessions, many models are booked directly from books or poster sheets. Sometimes models are requested for a go-see or asked to have their comps submitted because their face was seen in the book or on the poster.

Direct Bookings

Models usually get bookings through agents, but they can also be hired directly by photographers or art directors without an agent. There are pros and cons to being booked directly for a job. On the positive side, when models are booked directly they do not have to pay an agent any commission. And talking directly with the photographer or art director means there is less chance of any confusion about the particulars of the job (time, directions, wardrobe, etc.).

However, a model who is booked without an agent has little recourse if he or she is not paid. Legal action is always a possibility, however the model must determine if the time and money invested in the legal proceedings is worthwhile.

Before taking any direct bookings, make sure you have a firm understanding of the business end of modeling. It is easy to lose money due to lack of information. Your agent can negotiate and get the proper fees, and knows if any bonuses are applicable to the job.

If you take a direct booking, make sure whoever is being billed for the job (the photographer, advertising agency, or client) signs a voucher or a similar document after the session. A voucher is a bill and contract, which is discussed in more detail later in Chapter 9: "How to Work as a Professional Model." When booking through an agent, the model does not have to submit invoices to the client or act as a bill collector if the payment is late.

Don't underestimate the work involved in bill collecting. I once had a job with a client from Europe. I was paid within 90 days for the travel days (getting to and from the shoot), but I was not paid the bonus fee or for the actual shooting day. I spoke with my agent and was told that the photographer was having some financial problems. Another month went by. My agent told me that the photographer would start paying in monthly installments. The photographer paid his first month's installment, but no check arrived for the next month. I asked my agent what should be done. She said that she had worked with the photographer for many years, and believed that he would eventually pay. My agent made many, many calls, and sent dozens of letters. It took one year, but I was eventually paid in full. Agents generally have a working history with photographers and advertising agencies. They know when to push to have a check sent and when to wait.

Occasionally, models are unable to collect their fee for a job. This should be a rare experience. Only once have I not been paid for a job, and that was because the client went bankrupt. Sometimes a company that goes bankrupt opens up again under a different name. If that happens, do not work for them again until you have been paid-in-full for your previous work.

Neither photographers, ad agencies, nor clients want to have the reputation of not paying their bills. If an agent is not paid, he or she can and should refuse to allow any of his or her models to do any future work with that client.

Good agents are knowledgeable and selective about who their models work with. If you get a call from someone wanting to book you directly and you have any doubts about their legitimacy or intent, you should definitely refer them to your agent. Let your agent make sure the person is really in the advertising industry.

9

How To Work As A Professional Model

What is Expected of a Professional Model

Make sure you look like you. Photographers have told me horror stories of models who are cast from their composite sheet, and then show up on the set looking like a different person. That is one of the problems that can occur with airbrushing, or computer programs used to remove scars or wrinkles from your photos. You must have pictures on your composite sheet that are up to date and accurately represent your appearance. It is fine to have your photos re-touched, if you can properly apply makeup to cover up everything that was removed from the photo. I have known models who were fired when they arrived at the photographer's studio because they had misrepresented their looks. You may actually hurt your chances of being cast by hiding your distinctive characteristics.

Depending on how quickly your physical appearance changes, adult composite sheets should generally be updated every two years. Some children might need them changed more frequently. The best rule to follow is that you should get new photos made when your old ones no longer look like you. If you undergo any physical changes, such as extreme hair style or color changes or weight gain or loss, you must notify your agent. This is especially true if you made a physical change after attending a go-see where you were booked for the job.

I learned a very valuable but painful lesson about a change of appearance. I went to a go-see for a national ad campaign. A week after the go-see, I accepted a two-week booking for the U.S. Navy. I had to get a haircut for the job, not a buzz cut—but a pretty conservative look. The following week I was told I had gotten the national ad. I took the train to New York, went to the studio and met the photographer. He asked me if I had cut my hair. I told him yes. He looked at my hair again and told me that it was too short for the ad. They found someone else that morning to replace me. I felt awful about losing the job and very embarrassed about the situation. I should have told my agent that I had cut my hair before going to the shoot. I will never make that mistake again.

■　■　■　■　■

Be Responsible

Once you agree to attend a go-see, you must show up. If for any reason you can't attend, tell your agent. The client is expecting to see the requested models and a number of others. The client is spending a lot of money, and wants to have a lot of choices in order to decide who is perfect for the job. If the client or photographer requested to see you, then it will create tension between the client, photographer, and your agent if you do not show up. This will not help your relationship with your agent.

Never show up late to a job or a go-see. It makes you and your agent look bad. If it happens enough times, your agent will not submit you and photographers will not request you.

Being late for a job sets up an uncomfortable atmosphere. I was at a shoot where the model I was to work with was not on time. Everyone was waiting: the photographer, the client, the stylist, the art director, the copywriter the assistant photographer, and the account executive. Not only did the model cause the project to cost thousands of dollars more, but he also created a very tense atmosphere on the set. Neither the photographer nor I could experiment and try out creative ideas. There was a limited budget and a limited amount of time for shooting. Because so much time was lost waiting for the model, everything was rushed. The photographer had to go with a very straightforward traditional shot. Everyone was very unhappy, including me.

I have heard models say, "What is the big deal about showing up a little late? Most of the time you have to sit and wait for the photographer anyway." That can be true. Many times you sit and wait for the photographer, but it is your responsibility to show up on time. Don't forget, you are getting paid extremely well to sit and wait. Showing up late makes everyone in the modeling profession look bad.

Give yourself plenty of time to get to a job. Allow extra time in case you get lost, hit traffic, or have parking problems. If you happen to show up very early, go inside and let someone know you have arrived. Ask where you can hang up your wardrobe and find out where you should wait. Leave the photographer alone. He or she might be prepared to shoot right away or could be incredibly stressed out because of a technical problem. You will be told when the photographer is ready. If you are running late for a job, call your agent to inform him or her when you will arrive on the set, and to find out if you still have the booking.

Sometimes being late is simply out of your control. Once I had two morning go-sees in New York. I gave myself plenty of time to attend both castings. My train was an hour late and still I had time for both go-sees. After the first go-see, I took the subway to get to the second one. But someone had pulled the emergency brake on one of the subway cars and I had to wait a half hour for the next train. The 10-minute trip turned into a 45-minute adventure. The second casting ended at 12:00

and it was 12:15 by the time I arrived. My point is: sometimes you have no control over your arrival time. Always give yourself extra time. Even with bad luck, you still may be able to keep your appointments.

You Were Hired to Model

It is very important to remember why you are on the set. It is because you were chosen to be a model in an ad. The set is not the place to try and sell any products or services you might also be involved with. If someone asks you about any other jobs you might have, you need not shy away from answering, but do not walk on the set with samples of cosmetics or other products that you are trying to sell. The people who have hired you do not want to deal with anything else except getting a great photo with you. This also holds true with discussing family problems or scheduling difficulties. Focus on your modeling work.

Wardrobe

Part of your high hourly fee goes towards being prepared with the proper wardrobe. Double-check the wardrobe list you got from your agent or stylist to make sure you have everything. Don't skimp on bringing clothes. Sometimes you feel more like a moving company than a model because of all the things you are hauling to the shoot. If you bring more clothes, the photographer has more choices. Even if a stylist is bringing some clothing, you still might want to bring wardrobe that is appropriate for the shoot. That can translate into a better-looking shot, which will help you get future jobs.

If a model only brings one shirt, one tie and one suit for a business shot, the photographer will not have any options. If the colors or styles are not right for the shot, then you are cheating yourself out of a possible great tear sheet and an enjoyable experience with the photographer. The photographer can try to get another suit, which will take a lot of time, or just go with what the model brought and not be very happy about the look.

I was on a shoot where the other model brought one shirt and one tie that were identical to mine. Fortunately, I brought a few extra pieces of wardrobe. The photographer would not have been very happy to have two models wearing the same clothes. Bring a wide variety of clothing so wardrobe is never an issue at a shoot.

Don't forget all the accessories that go along with the wardrobe. Always dress from head to toe. If you are asked to look like a business person, don't forget a watch. If you are to be a husband or wife, don't forget a wedding ring. Bring as many accessories as possible. And don't be surprised if, after lugging two garment bags of wardrobe into the studio, the photographer says that what you are wearing is just perfect. It happens often.

Unless specifically requested, you should avoid clothing that is white, red, and black—these colors generally do not photograph well. This is true for black and white, as well as, color photos. Think about undergarments as well. Don't wear a white or off-white blouse and a red or black bra, or light-colored pants and black or red underwear. Wear white or off-white undergarments.

How To Get Wardrobe You Do Not Own

If you do not own the wardrobe you've been asked to bring to a shoot, there are five things you can do:

1. Ask your agent if the photographer or stylist can supply the wardrobe.
2. Borrow the items from friends or relatives.
3. Purchase and keep the wardrobe.
4. Purchase the clothing from a consignment shop, then, if desired, resell it back to the store.
5. Ask a store manager if clothes can be borrowed for a shoot and returned after the session. In return the store may get a name credit in the ad. Before offering the name credit idea to the store manager, get an agreement in writing from someone at the ad agency.

Food and Wardrobe Do Not Mix

If you take a lunch break during a shoot, make sure you don't spill any food or drinks on the wardrobe. The best thing to do is change your clothes. If that is not possible, find something to put on top of the wardrobe—perhaps an apron or a large towel.

Be careful about wrinkling the wardrobe or doing anything to it that changes its original appearance. Just use some common sense.

Think Before You Speak

If you think the wardrobe chosen for you looks ridiculous, don't go around saying, "What idiot picked out this garbage?" You were cast to look a certain way. You may not understand the concept of the ad or where or how it is being marketed. Someone invested a lot of time trying to figure out exactly how you should be dressed.

When to Put on Makeup

Unless you are told otherwise, do not put on makeup or put anything in your hair before arriving for a shoot. If the look is not what the photographer or art director wants, then a lot of time will be wasted in removing it.

You or the makeup artist will put on your makeup after the photographer or stylist selects your wardrobe and describes the kind of makeup he or she wants. Generally you will be dressed in your wardrobe before putting on makeup. This helps prevent smearing the makeup and staining the clothes.

On the Set

Stay in position. When you first walk on the set, you will be told where to stand. The photographer will then look through the camera to see if the shot is framed correctly and if the lighting looks right. It is important to stay in one position, because if you move after the lighting is set, the shot might not look right. If you get tired being in one position, just ask the photographer for a break. Before moving, make sure there is a piece of tape or something on the floor marking your position.

Not all shots are done with the model in one position. Standing still could be inappropriate for certain shots.

Do Not Touch The Props

Sometimes the set is filled with props. Don't play with the props. Positioning is crucial to the shot; if something gets moved even a few inches, it could make the difference between the ad looking real or staged. If an important prop is broken, the shoot might have to stop. Sometimes you need to have a prop moved in order to get in a certain position. If you notice a prop move while shooting, tell the photographer. It might not matter, but the information could be helpful.

You might be asked to hold a prop, especially if the item is the selling point of the ad. If you are using a prop, be careful with it.

Getting Information About the Ad

Before the shoot begins, make sure you have studied and understand the layout of the ad. Ask the art director and/or photographer about the kind of look, feeling and expression they want. If you are unsure about the ad's message, ask questions. It is crucial that you understand the ad and how it needs to be delivered. Without this information, you will be lost. The camera becomes your worst enemy. It will pick up the vacancy and uncertainty in your eyes. Think of ways to get the needed expressions.

This is where your acting training is very helpful.

It is your responsibility to know how to deliver the look needed to make the shot perfect. Once you feel ready, just relax, create, and have a good time.

Getting Conflicting Information about the Ad

The photographer or art director generally supplies the model with information about the ad. But you may be confused if you get conflicting suggestions and comments from the photographer, art director, and even the client. In this situation, talk to the photographer privately. Tell the photographer about the conflicting messages and ask what you should do. The photographer might be completely unaware that other people were giving you different ideas about the shot.

Sometimes you are working with people who have big egos and are used to having their way. The client is spending a lot of money, so it is essential that everyone is pleased with the photo session. Art directors make their living by having things look a certain way. Photographers get rehired because their photos look great. Everyone has a lot at stake. Everyone needs to be heard, but generally it is the photographer who should be listened to. Most of the time the photographer is the link between the client, art director, and the model.

Never Discuss Fees

Never discuss fees with the other models, photographers, ad agency people, or the client while you are working. Now is the time to concentrate on your work. It is your agent's job to deal with money. All discussions about fees should have been ironed out prior to the shoot. Two models working on the same set may get different fees due to their experience or longer travel time getting to the job. I've seen models get so involved in arguments that they were not able to concentrate on their work. Fees are a private matter between you and your agent. If you need or want to talk about fees, wait until after the session is completed.

Do Not Discuss Upgrades While Working

An upgrade is given to a model when his or her ad is placed in a high-exposure format. For example, billboard ads receive more exposure than ads running in a newspaper, and are therefore considered upgrades. Appearing on a billboard can closely identify you with a product, which could prevent you from doing an ad for a competitor even years after the ad ran. Because of the overexposure you might lose work in areas where the billboards are located. An upgrade could mean thousands of additional dollars.

Let Your Agent Renegotiate Fees

Renegotiating fees is not your job. Let your agent work for his or her percentage. It is easy to be paranoid and think everyone is trying to rip you off. Sometimes what seems like an effort to rip you off is actually a mistake due to lack of communication. Once I was in a situation where my agent told me my ad would appear in a newspaper only. But on the set I heard that it was also going to be used on billboards. I finished the shoot. Before I signed the voucher I called my agent to tell her about the change in usage. She spoke with the photographer, and I simply wrote the new information on the voucher. It was taken care of very easily. If I didn't do a good job, the client might not have liked the finished product and scrapped the entire billboard idea, or they could have kept the billboard idea and reshot it with a different model. Be professional and concentrate on your work.

The Voucher

When the shoot is over, you will be asked to sign a voucher. A voucher is a bill and a contract. It must be signed by the model and the person who will be billed for the job (that means the person who is paying). Always bring a few vouchers to each session. If you were booked directly for the job, an agent's voucher can be used. Scratch out the agent's name and put your name, address, and phone number on the voucher. Each agent has his or her own voucher, which should contain the following information:

- Name of model agency
- Name of model
- Date job was done
- Hours of job
- Hourly fee
- Name of photographer
- Who gets billed for the job (the photographer or ad agency)
- Explanation of usage for the ad—e.g. billboard, point of-purchase (a display ad in a store to promote the sale of a product), brochure, newspaper, poster, packages, etc.
- Time length of usage (Time usage begins after the photo is published, not after the date of session.)
- Name of the product

AGENT'S NAME, ADDRESS, PHONE NUMBER

INVOICE TO				MODEL				
ADDRESS				PHOTOGRAPHER				
CITY	STATE		ZIP	BOOKING DATE	FROM	TO	RATE	AMOUNT
ATTENTION				OTHER				AMOUNT
ACCOUNT (a)	PRODUCT (b)			PURCHASE ORDER/JOB NO.				SUB TOTAL

MEDIA USAGE (REPRODUCTION/LICENSING RIGHTS)

	National	Regional	Local			
Consumer Mag. #				☐ Double Page	☐ Album Cover	☐ Brochure
Consumer Newsp. #				☐ Single Page	☐ Photomatic	☐ Catalog
Trade Mag. #				☐ 1/2 Page	☐ Editorial	☐ Packaging
Trade Newsp. #				☐ Poster	☐ Annual Report	☐ Point of Pur.
				☐ Test_____	☐ Billboard	☐ Transit
				☐ Television	☐ Book Cover	☐ Other

SERV. CHG. 20%

EXPENSES

TOTAL

PERIOD OF USE:

In consideration of the sum stated hereon, I hereby sell, assign and grant to above or those for whom they are acting as indicated above, the right and permission to copyright and/or use and/or publish photographic portraits or pictures of me in which I may be included in whole or in part or composite or reproductions thereof in color or otherwise made through any media at their studios or elsewhere for art, advertising, trade or any other similar lawful purpose whatsoever, except on television, for a period terminating TWELVE (12) months from date hereof.

I hereby waive my right to inspect and/or approve the finished product or the advertising copy that may be used in connection therewith. I hereby release and discharge the above, its successors and all persons acting under its permission or authority or those for whom it is acting from any liability by virtue of any blurring, distortion, alteration, optical illusion or use in composite form that may occur or be produced in the taking of said picture or in processing tending toward the completion of the finished product.

NOTE: These photographs may be used only by the account (a), for the product (b), and in the manner (c) specified above. They may not be used for packages, point-of-purchase displays, billboards or posters unless a bonus payment is included. Neither this nor any other release is valid until payment in full is received by McDONALD/RICHARDS, INC. **TERMS: NET 30 DAYS.** A monthly finance charge of 1 1/2 percent will be applied to all invoices not paid within 30 days.

THIS RELEASE TAKES PRECEDENCE OVER ANY RELEASE SIGNED AT THE TIME OF JOB WITH EXCEPTION OF CONTRACTS AND AGENCY RELEASES THAT CONTAIN THE SAME INFORMATION HEREIN.

CLIENT'S SIGNATURE   DATE   MODEL'S SIGNATURE   DATE

Sample voucher

Many vouchers have three color-coded copies. The model, agent, and the person to be billed each get one copy. Keep your copy in a convenient and safe place. File your vouchers in chronological order, so that you can easily see if any payments are overdue. For example, I did a job in 1989, then in 1991 I noticed the ad running in *People* magazine. I checked my records for 1989 and found the shooting date. Knowing the date made it easy to find a voucher that was two years old. The voucher showed a 12-month usage agreement. Since it ran past the 12 months and I could produce our original agreement (with the voucher), my agent was able to collect another payment for the ad. Models often lose money due to sloppy handling of their vouchers.

Computing the Time for the Voucher

When a model gets a confirmed booking, he or she will be told the hours of the shoot. Models can also be booked by the day or days. If your session goes longer than expected, your agent may have you bill in 15-minute increments (some to the next half-hour). That means if you were booked for a three hour shoot and it lasted three hours and 20 minutes, then you would charge for a three and one half hour session. Below is a simple chart that shows you the quarterly hour fees in relation to your hourly fee. You should copy this and bring it with you on all shoots. This chart will make it easy to figure out the full amount of money owed to you as you write it in the voucher.

If you are making:

$250 an hour, then you are being paid $62.50 every 15 minutes.

$200 an hour, then you are being paid $50.00 every 15 minutes.

$150 an hour, then you are being paid $37.50 every 15 minutes.

$125 an hour, then you are being paid $31.25 every 15 minutes.

$100 an hour, then you are being paid $25.00 every 15 minutes.

It is not a common practice, but if you are asked to change the finish time of a shoot by a few minutes in order to lower the cost of the session, there are a few things you can do.

■ Insist on being paid for the time worked.

■ Check with your agent before agreeing to the request.

■ Say they must negotiate directly with your agent.

Once, I was working on a national ad campaign. The job was supposed to be a 2-plus-1 (a two-hour booking with a one-hour "hold"). That means the model must leave an additional hour open in case the shoot takes more than two hours to complete. However, this job took more than five hours. There were many delays because the client, art director, and copywriter were not able to agree on many things. We shot past 5:30 p.m., which is considered overtime according to my New York agent. When we were finished, the photographer, whom I have worked with many times, said, "The advertising agency will go crazy when they get the bill." I told the photographer if it would make it easier for him, I would forget about the overtime, and he could just pay me straight time. The photographer told me that I should get paid for my work and that it was not my fault we went into overtime. I mentioned it to my agent, and she was very upset with me. She told me that it was her job to negotiate. That is why she is getting 20 percent commission on my jobs. I do not offer reductions anymore without first clearing it with my agent.

The Model Release

After the session, you might be asked to sign a model release form. Signing this document means that you release your rights to the usage, design, or the overall image of the photograph. Read the model release carefully. It always says the photograph can be used in "any or all media," and for "any purpose whatsoever," or words to that effect. In the sample adult model release form I have printed those words in bold. Never sign it without scratching out the words, "any or all media" and "for any other purpose whatsoever." Next, you should write in exactly how the ad will be used. For example, "in newspaper only," "brochure only," etc. Then initial it and sign it. By signing the model release without any changes, you are giving the ad agency permission to use the ad on TV, billboards, point of purchase, or through any form of advertising, without being paid additional fees.

ADULT MODEL RELEASE

In consideration of my engagement as a model, and for other good and valuable consideration herein acknowledged as received, upon the terms hereinafter stated, I hereby grant _____, his legal representatives and assigns, those for whom _____ is acting, and those acting with his authority and permission, the absolute right and permission to copyright and use, reuse and publish, and republish photographic portraits or pictures of me or in which I may be included, in whole or in part, or composite or distorted in character or form, without restriction as to changes or alterations, from time to time, in conjunction with my own or a fictitious name, or reproductions thereof in color or otherwise *made through any media* at his studios or elsewhere for art, advertising, trade, or *any other purpose whatsoever*. I also consent to the use of any printed matter in conjunction therewith. I hereby waive any right that I may have to inspect or approve the finished product or products or the advertising copy or printed matter that may be used in connection therewith or the use to which it may be applied.

I hereby release, discharge and agree to save harmless _____ his legal representatives or assigns, and all persons acting under his permission or authority or those for whom he is acting, from any liability by virtue of any blurring, distortion, alteration, optical illusion, or use in composite form, whether intentional or otherwise, that may occur or be produced in the taking of said picture or in any subsequent processing thereof, as well as any publication thereof even though it may subject me to ridicule, scandal, reproach, scorn and indignity.

I hereby warrant that I am of full age and have every right to contract in my own name in the above regard. I state further that I have read the above authorization, release and agreement, prior to its execution, and that I am fully familiar with the contents thereof.

Name:_____ Witness: _____

Address:_____

Date: _____

A release form for minors has the same information as an adult. The only difference is an additional section for the parent or guardian to sign the document.

Do not sign anything you do not understand even if other people are doing it. Just tell the photographer that some things are unclear and your agent likes to read everything you are asked to sign. Some agents request to have the model release form faxed to them before their model signs it.

Asking for a Tear Sheet

After the voucher and model release forms are signed, ask the art director if you can get a copy of the ad after it is completed. If the art director is not on the set, then get the name of the art director from the photographer. This is an essential part of the modeling business; you need new tear sheets to put together new composite sheets or update your mini book. It can be harder to get the tear sheet than the booking. You must be persistent but not obnoxious. Sometimes the art director will ask for your address and tell you that he or she will send you a copy when things are completed, but art directors are very busy, and most of the time they will forget to send you a tear sheet. So always ask when the ad will be completed, then ask if you can call at that time to remind him or her about getting a copy.

The Problems with Tear Sheets on Newspaper

Whenever possible try to avoid getting your tear sheet from the newspaper. It will not reproduce well on a composite sheet or look good in your mini book. Laminating the newspaper will help slow the yellowing process, but it will still fade over time. If the ad is only running in newspapers, see if you can also get an 8 x 10 photo from the session. Even though it won't have all the information or copy that makes it look like an ad, it is better to have a nice sharp image for reproduction purposes than an ad that looks aged. If a few 8 x 10's were produced from the session, sometimes you can get one of the outakes for free. Quite often the shot that is used for the ad is the best shot, so expect to pay the photographer $10 or $15 for a black and white copy. It is always in your best interest to use the best shot available. If the shot is in color you should expect to pay more. Unlike ads in newspaper, magazine and brochure ads generally reproduce well and last a long time.

When to Show Your Book or Comp

After the shoot and paperwork is completed, ask the photographer and art director if they would like to look at your mini book and composite sheet.

Ask if it is helpful for you to leave a comp. If you were selected from an agent's book, it is possible that neither the art director nor the photographer has ever seen your comp or mini book.

Information Needed From Every Job

Before leaving the set or location, make sure you have the following information recorded for yourself in a record book.

- Date of job
- Hours worked
- Location of shoot
- Name of agent who booked you the job
- Photographer: name, address, phone number
- Advertising agency: name, address, phone number
- Art director: name, address, phone number
- Copy writer: name, address, phone number
- Makeup artist: name, address, phone number
- Stylist or prop person: name, address, phone number
- Name of product (or job number)
- Type of character you portrayed
- Who to contact to get a tear sheet, and when the ad will be completed
- Notes about any unusual circumstances

You always want to present yourself as an experienced and professional model. Think about the long term. You are building relationships along the way. Every negative experience could hurt your chances of working. Every positive experience could mean more work in the future.

The Work After the Work

1. After the job, call your agent to report the hours you worked. This immediately starts the billing process.
2. Mail the agent's copy of the voucher that same day.
3. Make a note in your calendar of when you should call or send a letter to the photographer or art director requesting a tear sheet.
4. Write a message in your calendar 90 days after the job to make sure you have been paid. (The main reason the model has to wait so long for payment is because the model is the last person to get paid. The client pays the advertising agency, the advertising agency pays the photographer, the photographer pays the agent, and the agent pays the model. Sometimes the client is billed directly by the agent in which case the model might get paid sooner. Even if the photographer is being billed for the job, he or she normally will not pay the agent until he or she is paid.)
5. Record and file all the important information concerning the job in a book (date, name of agent, photographer, art director, etc.).
6. Keep a list of your mileage and any expenses that were job related. They could be tax deductible.
7. If appropriate, send a composite sheet (for their files) and a note to the photographer and art director to say that you enjoyed working with them.

Keep All of Your Vouchers Together

If payment is not received within 90 days, call or send a note to your agent. Never call anyone but your agent concerning an overdue bill. Give your agent all of the relevant information. Remember, your agent is working with hundreds or possibly thousands of models. The more information you give him or her, the quicker your agent can find out about a delayed payment.

Keep another list of when you get paid. Write "paid in full" on your voucher and date it. When someone mails you a tear sheet, send a thank-you note.

Turning Down Jobs

There are times when your ethics or other considerations make it appropriate for you to decline a booking, but think very carefully before turning down a job.

Personal Reasons

If you do not want to be associated with a certain product, don't accept the booking. I got a call from an art director about doing a job dealing with child abuse. It sounded like a very powerful and well-thought-out campaign. The message was that even regular—looking people—your friendly, kind, next-door-neighbor-type of person – could be a child abuser. I had mixed feelings about the ad. I liked the concept, and thought it would be helpful to get that kind of information out to people. But I turned it down because I did not want to be associated with being a child abuser. I would not want my children or their friends to see me in that type of ad. I was also concerned about the possibility of losing work because of the connection with that type of character.

Doing a cigarette ad can be a difficult decision for some people. If you don't want to support cigarettes but are offered $12,000 to do an ad, it can be a tough choice. You could dislike the product, but still decide to accept the booking. I knew a model who hated cigarettes, but did a national cigarette campaign and donated most of the proceeds to the American Cancer Society. If you are offered a job advertising a product you do not wish to be associated with, seriously consider turning it down. Your affiliation with that product could haunt you for years.

Financial Reasons

You might get a call to do a job, but the client can only pay $50 an hour instead of your normal $75 or $100 per hour. Some models automatically refuse jobs when they are offered a lower-than-normal hourly fee. Taking a job at a lower fee could make it more difficult to get your regular fee for future jobs.

Before making a decision, find out if the shot would be good for your portfolio. Are the photographer and art director new contacts for you? If so, you might consider it a way of getting paid to introduce yourself to them. Also, you never know how long a shoot might last. I've been booked for a 1-plus-1 and the shoot lasted three to four hours. And you never know who you might meet on a set. I met a model at a low-paying job who introduced me to an agent in another market I was unfamiliar with. I contacted the new agent and have been working with her for years.

When I was just getting started in the business I actually lost money on a job due to my agent's fees and transportation costs. I viewed it as a long-term investment. I knew that I would do a great job and if a future project came up that I was right for I would be requested.

Sometimes models are hired as *extras* on a shoot. They are considered *extras* because their faces are not clearly seen in the shot, or because they are in the background.

There is no specific fee established for *extra* work. Instead of the model being paid an hourly fee, generally a flat rate is paid. The fees paid to the model can vary from $50 to $500 for the shoot.

If you are asked to do *extra* work, you should seriously consider taking the job. I have seen people get upgraded from an *extra* to a principal. Also, it gives you the opportunity to learn more about photo sessions, meet photographers and art directors, and network with other models.

Before accepting or rejecting a booking, get the necessary information, think about what is best for you, and then decide.

Two Agents—Two Bookings—Same Day

If you freelance with different agents and are booked for a job through agent X and another job comes in from agent Y for the same day, what do you do? Normally you would turn the second job down because you are already booked. But what if the first job is a three-hour booking that would pay hundreds of dollars, and the second job is a national ad campaign that would pay thousands of dollars?

The best approach in this situation is to be honest. Explain the situation to agent X, and ask if the shooting date or perhaps the times could be changed to accommodate both jobs. If not, ask agent X if it is possible to get you released from the first booking. Quite often the agents are understanding and can work things out to help you get the more lucrative job.

Keep in mind what you are asking agent X to do. He or she will have to explain to the client why you are no longer available, and spend more time finding a replacement and making sure the client is happy with the other choice. The agent could lose his or her commission if the client decides to get a model from a different agency.

If the agent cannot get you out of the smaller job, keep your commitment and decline the national ad. I have heard stories of models lying to their agent in order to keep a more lucrative job. They accepted both jobs, then called in sick to the less profitable job. One agent told me about a model who was in that situation and simply did not show up for the smaller job.

Lying to an agent or not showing up for a job is a bad way of doing business. Agents will not represent people they can not trust or rely on. In this industry, as in any industry, you must think about the long term. Don't do things that will sever a relationship with an agent with whom you work regularly. You may lose money by taking the smaller job, but it's worth a lot more to have an agent that trusts and respects your word and integrity.

When to Call an Agent

Always ask agents about their phone call policy. Find out if they want you to call periodically, or send notes or postcards in order to stay in touch with them. Many agents prefer that you send post cards every two months or so. This is a good way to remind the agent that you are still around. Describe what you have worked on lately (theater, TV commercials, radio, classes, etc.). Listing recent projects is a good way to let the agent know that you are marketable. Do not try to stay in contact with an agent by barging into his or her office and beginning to discuss world events.

Unless you have something urgent to discuss, like a job-related problem, set up an appointment. This way the agent can give you his or her undivided attention. It is very important to have a good line of communication.

When You Are Unavailable for Work

If you are working with one agent, make sure the agent knows when you are unavailable for work. Because of last-minute calls about bookings, it is important that your agent knows your schedule. If you are working with a number of agents and will be unavailable for seven or more days due to a booking, vacation, or for any reason, make sure they have the dates.

While on vacation, try to check in with your answering machine daily. It is important to get away from work, but you are the only one running your business. If calls come in, you are the only one who can handle them. You could lose a great booking by not listening to messages. It also makes things hard for your agent who might be desperately trying to reach you.

If you are requested for a job, your agent has to get back to the photographer or art director to let them know that he or she can't reach you. If it is a last-minute job, your agent might get bombarded with phone calls from the photographer or art director throughout the day as they scramble around trying to quickly put together a shoot. They will need to know if there is any new information about the model's availability. It makes the agent look bad if he or she cannot reach you. The model and agent could lose the booking if the photographer or art director can't wait any longer, and book a model through a different agent. When you are not at home, make sure you check in for messages.

How to Speak to an Agent When Work Is Slow

Do not call or stop into an agent's office demanding to know why he or she has not gotten you any work. That approach is never in your best interest. If you are not getting much work, there are better ways to approach an agent.

If your agent is submitting your comps to potential clients and you are still not getting any work, set up an appointment and talk with your agent. Make sure you are being considered for the right jobs. Ask if you need to change your comp. Try to get some concrete suggestions on what you can do to get more work. Remember, it is in the agent's best interest to get you bookings. That is how the agent makes a living.

Additional Modeling Fees

On top of the hourly fee, additional monies are paid for certain high-exposure usages such as:

- Billboards   ■ Point of purchase   ■ Displays   ■ Posters   ■ Packages
- Exclusivity   ■ Usage longer than 12 or 24 months

Some agencies charge an overtime fee if the booking is on a

- Holiday
- Weekend
- If the hours worked are before 9:00 a.m. or after 5:30 p.m.

Sometimes there are special rates for travel days, full-day bookings, prep time, and the wearing of lingerie and transparent apparel. Prep time is the time needed for special preparation before a photo session. Once I was cast to be the "Big Bad Wolf," and the makeup artist needed three hours to put my makeup on and 45 minutes to take the makeup off. Sometimes models are paid one half the normal hourly fee for prep time.

Photo by Bruce Weller—Fallano/Faulkner & Associates
Makeup Frank Rogers

10

The Realities Of Being A Full-Time Model

Being Self Employed

Although models are submitted for jobs by agents, they are considered to be self-employed. There are many benefits to being your own boss. For example, you decide how hard you want to work. I know many people who model part time, get a few bookings a year, and are extremely happy with their modeling situation. Others pursue modeling as their full-time occupation and can earn $20,000 to $40,000 or more annually.

SAG, AFTRA, and AEA withhold money from each paycheck for taxes, and offer health and pension benefits to those who qualify. There is a new union for modeling called The Models Guild. Hopefully, in the near future they will offer similar benefits to models.

Models are fully responsible for their own insurance. Commercial models have no taxes withheld from their paycheck. Talk to an accountant to make sure you are saving enough money to pay your taxes, and have money for retirement.

Is Commercial Modeling for You?

I truly love my work, but there are aspects about the business that I don't always like. It can be demoralizing, frustrating, frightening, and stressful. It can also be exhilarating, wonderful, and an extremely rewarding profession. As in any job, in order to be successful, you must be willing to work hard. Also, as in any job, hard work does not guarantee success. And remember, the competition is strong.

When I began, I decided not to have any goals for my first year. I just wanted to experience the work and the life-style to see how it felt. I am not saying you should not have goals, but before goals are set, first find out if modeling is something you really enjoy. Make sure that an uncertain income is something you and perhaps your spouse and family can handle. Most important, make sure you love the work.

■ ■ ■ ■ ■

If modeling interests you, try it. It is always sad for me to hear people say they wished they had tried modeling, but now it's too late. Whether you are successful or not, if you try you will not have to look back and wonder how far you could have gone in the field. Even if you only get one booking in your entire life, it will be well worth the effort. Being photographed professionally is an incredible experience—one that will last you a lifetime.

Start off part-time in your community, and see what it is like. Do not try moving to any large market without experience. It is very expensive to live in New York, Los Angeles, Miami, or Chicago and they can be tough places to get started. If you already live in one of those markets, find small agencies to begin with.

You can get great tear sheets and lots of training in your own community. If your area does not have much commercial modeling work, find the closest city that does.

After you have worked enough to get some wonderful photos, put your comp together. If you have enough material, get a mini-book started. After those projects are completed, begin seeking representation in a major market.

I hope my stories and experience have given you a greater understanding and insight into the workings of the commercial modeling industry. I hope your career brings you great satisfaction, as mine has for me. Good luck to you.

Feel free to send me questions pertaining to commercial modeling. If your question is used in my upcoming "Commercial Modeling Newsletter," you will receive one free issue.

Please remember to include your address and phone number so I can contact you! Mail your questions or comments to:

MARCUS INSTITUTE OF COMMERCIAL MODELING
AARON MARCUS—Director
P.O. Box 32564
Baltimore, Maryland U.S.A. 21282-2564
(410) 764-8270 Fax (410) 764-5636 e-mail bk@howtomodel.com
web site: http://www.howtomodel.com

11

Now What Do You Do?

1. Learn how to show many different expressions in a believable way. Take acting lessons. Try to do some theater.
2. Practice different looks and expressions in front of a camera.
3. Contact agents.
4. Decide on your image.
5. Find a photographer and have your head shot photos taken.
6. Show the contact sheets to an agent or agents.
7. Get copies made of your head shot.
8. Write your resume.
9. Send your headshot to agents, and try to get work.
10. Purchase and learn how to apply makeup.
11. Select the shots for your composite sheet.
12. Put your composite sheet together.
13. Mail composite sheets and head shots to photographers, art and creative directors at advertising agencies.
14. Purchase one mini book.
15. When you are ready to find representation in other markets, buy a Polaroid camera in order to photograph yourself and send the photos for the go-sees you are unable to attend.

12

Resources

Unions:

AEA
   Actors Equity Association (theater) AEA is a mixture of an open and non open union. If you have been a SAG or AFTRA member for over a year you can join AEA. The initiation fee is around $800, which can be paid over a period of time. The other ways of joining AEA are to be cast in an equity play and offered an equity contract (this is similar to being cast as a principal actor in a SAG production), or work as an equity membership candidate for fifty weeks in an equity play (this is similar but a lot longer than working three times as an extra in a SAG production).

ACTRA
   Association of Canadian Television and Radio Artists

AFTRA
   American Federation of Television and Radio Artists (radio and some TV commercials, soap operas, disk jockeys, news people). AFTRA is an open union, meaning anyone can join. The maximum initiation fee is almost $900, but it could be hundreds of dollars less depending on where you live.

SAG
   Screen Actors Guild (for movies, most TV commercials, some TV shows—if shot on film) SAG is not an open union. You must be cast as a principal character (important part) in a SAG production, or work three days as an extra to be eligible to join SAG. Like AFTRA, the initiation fee is dependent on where you live. The most expensive is the Washington, D.C. branch, which charges around $1,100. The fee is calculated at twice the current theatrical/TV day player rate.

THE MODELS GUILD
   Is designed to be a unified voice and protect the rights of models, photographers, stylists, hair and makeup artists and their reps, agents, managers, and bookers. They offer on-line portfolio services, career counseling services, health insurance and financial services. For additional information call 800-864-4696.

■ ■ ■ ■ ■

Other Helpful Books

"Headshot Photographer's Guide"
> Published by Ken Taranto Photo Services, Inc.
> This book lists names and shows head shots of many photographers.
> (800) 556-3914 or (212) 691-6070

"The Marcus Institute's National Directory of SAG & AFTRA Offices"
> Published by The Marcus Institute of Commercial Modeling

This valuable directory can help you get the names of hundreds of agents throughout the United States. Call the SAG or AFTRA office in the state desired, and ask for the list of signatory agents. These agents have agreed to abide by the SAG or AFTRA rules and regulations. Many represent commercial models and actors.

"The Marcus Institute's Industry Information Directory"

This special directory gives you names, address and phone numbers of companies that reproduce head shots and composite sheets, companies that sell mini-books, makeup and a list of New York and L.A. head shot photographers.

Each directory costs $15. Save $10 by purchasing both directories for only $19.95. Send a check or money order made payable to the Marcus Institute of Commercial Modeling (this fee includes shipping) to P.O. Box 32564, Baltimore, MD. 21282-2564. Maryland residents include $.75 for one directory and $1.00 for both (sales tax). Call the Marcus Institute for credit card orders.

Glossary Of Terms

Ad: Images and/or words used to help sell a product or idea.

AEA: (Actors Equity Association) Union for theater actors.

AFTRA: (American Federation of Television and Radio Artists) Union covering radio commercials, soap operas, disk jockeys, and news people.

Agency books: Publications that show photos of the models an agency represents.

Agency posters: Poster with head shots of the models represented by an agency.

Agent: A person who helps get models work.

Answering service: A company that takes phone messages.

Assistant photographer: A person who helps a photographer before, during, and after a photo session.

Art director: Person who helps create and design ads.

Base: The first layer of makeup used on ones face.

Billboard: A very large sign where ads are placed.

Body parts: Some models are cast because of their special features, such as hands, feet, legs, hair, etc.

Bonus: Payment of additional fees above the hourly rate. A bonus is received for high-exposure ads, such as: posters, point of purchase, billboards, packages, long term usage, exclusivity.

Booking: Getting hired for a job.

Call back: When models are called back to be seen again after the initial go-see.

■ ■ ■ ■ ■

Camera ready: 1. Art work that is ready for the printer. 2. When a model is ready to shoot with makeup and wardrobe on.

Cast: Being hired for a job.

Category: A group of models that has similar characteristics and features.

Catalog: A book or magazine showing different products.

Cattle call: When a large number of people attend a go-see or audition.

Cheating to the camera: Slightly turning the head and eyesight away from the person or object the model is working with and towards the camera lens. This technique gives the illusion that the model looking straight at the other person or object, and allows the camera to see more of the model's face.

Commercial modeling: Appearing in a still picture that promotes a product, or a company. People of all heights, ages, and sizes can work as commercial models.

Commission: A percentage of a model's earnings paid as a fee to an agent.

Composite sheet (comp):   A card with photographs showing the model's expressions and range.

Conflict: When a model has done an ad for a certain product, he or she avoids appearing in ads for competing products to avoid a conflict.

Contact sheet: Printed directly from negatives, a contact sheet shows in miniature all the pictures that were taken at a photo session.

Copy: The words of an ad.

Copy writer: Person who writes the words for an ad.

Creative director: Person who creates the concept of the ad and oversees and approves the project.

Crop: To adjust the shape and size of a photo.

Direct booking: When a model gets booked for a job without going through an agent.

Editorial shot: A photograph used to illustrate an article in a newspaper or magazine.

Exclusivity: When a model is represented by only one agent.

Exclusivity fee: Being paid to only work for one product or company.

Extra: When a model's face is not clearly recognizable or is only seen in the background of a photo.

Fee:	A monetary charge for a service.
Freelance:	Person who works with many agents.
Graphic artist:	Person who gets artwork ready for the printer.
Go-see:	A job audition for models.
Half body or 3/4 head shot:	A photograph that shows more of one's body than the typical head shot.
Head shot:	A close up photo of a person's head from the chest up.
Indigo:	A reproduction process that is superior to lasers and inferior to printing.
Job number:	A number assigned to an ad for billing and identification purposes.
Lamination:	A process of putting plastic covering over paper. Normally used for preservation purposes.
Laser:	A copying process where toner is used to reproduce a photo.
Layout:	A sample drawing of an ad, used as a guide for the photographer, stylist and prop person.
Loupe:	A small round magnifying device used to look at contact sheets and transparencies.
Makeup artist:	Person who puts makeup on models.
Mark:	Piece of tape on the floor showing the model's exact position.
Mini book:	A small portfolio book with tear sheets of a model's work.
Model form:	An information sheet that is filled out by models at a go-see.
Model release form:	A document giving a photographer or advertising agency full rights to a photo.
On location:	Shooting a photo outside the photographer's studio.
One plus one:	An hour-long booking with the possibility of working an additional hour.
Open call:	When an agent interviews new models.
Photo credit:	Putting the photographer's name next to his or her photo. This can be done on composite sheets, or in agency books.
Photomatic:	A slide presentation.
Point of purchase:	A display ad in a store.
Polaroid:	A camera that produces a print in less then 60 seconds.

Glossary Of Terms

Portfolio:	A compilation of a model's photos.
Powder:	Makeup used to take the shine off of one's face.
Prep time:	Time needed for special preparation before a session.
Profile:	A side view of the face.
Props:	Items used in a shot to make an ad look realistic.
Put on hold:	When a model is asked to reserve a specific date for the possibility of being booked.
Released:	When a model is told they are no longer being considered for a job.
Request:	When a model is specifically asked to appear for a casting.
Retouch:	To make a change on a photograph.
Right of first refusal:	When a model has been put on hold and a second job is offered for the same day. The person who originally put the model on hold has the right of first refusal. This person can either book or release the model.
Screen Actors Guild:	Union for actors cast in movies, certain TV commercials, and TV programs that are shot on film. (as opposed to being shot on video)
Session:	Another name for a photo shoot.
Shoot:	A photo session.
Sign-up sheet:	Sheet of paper for models to write their names and the names of their agents. It is used at go-sees so everyone knows who is next in line for the Polaroids.
Square to the camera:	When a model's face and body are facing straight into the lens.
Stock photography:	Generic photographs that can be used for many different purposes.
Stylist:	Person responsible for assembling wardrobe and sometimes props for a job.
Submittance:	When an agent mails photos in the hopes of getting bookings for their models.
Tear sheet:	A copy of an ad.
Test shot:	A photo used solely for a photographer's or model's portfolio.
Trade magazine:	A publication marketed to a specific field.

Transit:	Posters on vehicles, such as buses or subways.
Transparencies:	A slide that is larger than 35 millimeters.
Transparent apparel:	Clothing that can be seen through.
Travel reimbursement:	When a model is refunded the money spent for transportation to a shoot.
Travel time:	Getting paid for traveling. This occurs when a model travels a long distance getting to a job.
Type face:	The size and style of letters used in printing.
Upgrade:	When an ad is placed in a high exposure format, and the model receives an additional fee. When a model is promoted to a more prominent look in an ad.
Usage:	The length of time an ad will run.
Velox:	A high-contrast print on photo-sensitive paper.
Voucher:	The bill and contract that is used in the modeling industry.
Wardrobe:	Clothes that are used at a photo session.

About The Author

Aaron Marcus has been a professional actor and commercial model since 1984. As of this writing he is represented by 63 agents in many markets. He has been cast in 739 (to date) print ads, TV and radio commercials, industrial training and feature films, and network TV. Mr. Marcus has worked on commercial projects for companies such as: AT&T, McDonald's, StarKist Tuna, Acura, DuPont, Showtime, MCI, Campbell's, The Learning Channel, LifeSavers, Guinness Gold, Western Union, Red Roof Inn, Sunbeam, Hertz and K-Mart. His print ads have appeared throughout the United States, Europe and Asia, and have been seen in magazines such as: *Time*, *People*, *Newsweek*, *Reader's Digest*, *Parents*, *TV Guide*, *Sports Illustrated*, *Details*, *and Mirabella*.

Aaron Marcus has been seen on TV and in films such as *Broadcast News*, *Cry Baby*, *Stage Fright*, *America's Most Wanted*, and *General Lee*. He has been cast as a stand-in on projects such as *Silence of the Lambs*, *Homicide—Life On The Street*, *Guarding Tess*, and *The Pelican Brief*. He has worked on industrial training films for companies such as: The Discovery Channel, U.S. Navy, Bell Atlantic, IBM, NEA, Citicorp, MCI, and AARP.

Along with his modeling and acting, Aaron Marcus was a faculty member of The School for Film and Television at Three of Us Studios in New York, and has written commercial modeling articles for *Clique* magazine/Canada, *New Generation Magazine*/London, the Screen Actors Guild and The Models Guild.

Aaron Marcus has created the *How to Become a Successful Commercial Model Workshop*. This seminar is offered to schools, organizations and agencies throughout North America. For more information about Mr. Marcus' workshop, or newsletter, please contact The Marcus Institute of Commercial Modeling, Aaron Marcus, Director • P.O. Box 32564 • Baltimore, MD 21282-2564 • U.S.A. • (410) 764-8270, or e-mail bk@howtomodel.com
web site: http://www.howtomodel.com

■ ■ ■ ■ ■